M ichael dropped down He was obviously tire bed? Instead, he just sat and wa sheet off the light box, replaced it with a new one, and searched through it for shots she could use, then did it all again.

He finally roused himself. "What are you doing?"

She frowned. "You look awfully tired, Michael. Why don't you go home, go to bed?"

"No, I'm curious. Let me see." He came to sit beside her on the couch and leaned toward the light box.

He was very close. She could see the stitching on the collar of his shirt, could even smell the faint remnant of his after-shave. A surprisingly dark stubble was beginning to shadow his jaw, and from this angle she couldn't miss the line of muscles running from his shoulders, down his arm, and into his hands. His hands...Her breath caught. She knew those hands.

She jumped up and stumbled around the coffee table to the open floor beyond. "How about some ice cream? I found some incredible English chocolate sauce at a deli nearby, and there are some pecans in the freezer that I'm sure Lillian wouldn't mind sharing."

She pushed through the swinging door into the kitchen without waiting for his response. Forget friend, forget acquaintance—she had to get out of Singapore completely before she made a complete idiot of herself.

A PALISADES CONTEMPORARY ROMANCE

On ASSIGNMENT

Marilyn Kok

PALISADES

ON ASSIGNMENT
published by Palisades
a division of Multnomah Publishers, Inc.

©1998 by Marilyn Kok
International Standard Book Number: 1–57673–279–7

Cover illustration by Glenn Harrington
Design by Brenda McGee

Scripture quotations are from:
The Holy Bible, New International Version
©1973, 1984 by International Bible Society,
used by permission of Zondervan Publishing House

Palisades is a trademark of Multnomah Publishers, Inc.,
and is registered in the U.S. Patent and Trademark Office.

Printed in the United States of America

For information:
MULTNOMAH PUBLISHERS, INC.
POST OFFICE BOX 1720
SISTERS, OREGON 97759

98 99 00 01 02 03 04—10 9 8 7 6 5 4 3 2 1

For Randy, with love.

And for Leah, a kindred spirit and blessing from God.
You give my faith validity.

ACKNOWLEDGMENTS

In doing my research, God graciously provided people for me to talk to who have recently spent time in Singapore, chief among them Karen and Rod Evans, who contributed enormously to my understanding of life there, as well as Janet Friesen, Lisa Horn, Mikel Ann Pritz, and Denyse Gripentrog.

The Staley Library staff at Millikin University was kind enough to order dozens of books for me through interlibrary loan—thank you.

Thanks also to Michael Anthony Padulo for his *Kampong Capers*, his autobiographical description of an expatriate living with a Teochew family in Singapore.

And finally to Denise Gaskins, who has guided the development of my writing skills—when I've needed you most, you've been there, willing, gifted, and honest. Thank you.

The LORD your God is with you,
he is mighty to save.
He will take great delight in you,
he will quiet you with his love,
he will rejoice over you with singing.

ZEPHANIAH 3:17

ONE

Seeking shade from the burning afternoon sun, Tessa Brooks retreated to the trees that ran down Singapore's Orchard Road. Her flight from Japan had arrived shortly after noon. Given the choice of either unpacking or exploring, she'd put on her trademark White Sox baseball cap and headed straight for the door.

She had reason in the sun to appreciate the cap. She squirmed her shoulders to make a drop of sweat roll faster down her spine. How did the shoppers along the busy street move so quickly through this heat?

And yet if she could keep the humidity from ruining her film, she'd do fine here. Was there another city in Asia that was so immaculate? Clean and green: the travel brochures hadn't lied. With the right filters, she could moderate the blazing sunshine, and in late afternoon the horizontal light would warm the colors and make them even more vivid.

As for the other reason she had come —

She glanced at her watch. Four o'clock. Michael had left a message that he'd be coming by the hotel a little after five. How strange to think he might be in one of these buildings. He could be walking on a street nearby, perhaps on this very sidewalk.... She shook off the thought and turned back toward the hotel. She still had a little time to get herself ready before facing him.

But when the automatic doors opened, there he was, Michael Lawton himself, sitting across the lobby.

She instantly tensed.

At first glance, with his sandy-colored hair and even features, bent over what appeared to be a business report, he looked

9

incredibly ordinary. His hairline had begun receding—that was new, though of course, being Michael, he wasn't bothering to hide it—and over a slightly bulkier frame, he wore a typical banker's uniform: dress slacks, white shirt, and muted tie.

Nothing in his appearance to startle or confuse, and yet how misleading.

Late one afternoon four years ago, she had wheedled a sitting out of him and managed to catch on film the essence of Michael—the intelligence that lay behind the bland trappings, the incontestable self-assurance and strength of will. She could see that strength even now in the stillness of his gaze on the paper before him, the calm set of his shoulders, and the way he stroked his jaw. A worthy opponent on any field of battle—she should know.

She glanced down at her own plaid sundress, light and airy against the Singaporean heat, and winced. He might easily think it too short and frivolous, the kind of dress only a woman without obligations could wear.

She calmed herself. She wasn't here to prove anything to Michael Lawton. Just to herself.

She pulled off her cap, fluffed her hair, and set off across the lobby.

He smiled and stood, and she almost stumbled at his feet. He looked better than ever—it wasn't fair!. "Tessa." He took her hand in a steady grip, and she struggled to catch her breath. How could he be so relaxed? Wasn't he nervous at all?. "Welcome to Singapore."

"Thank you, Michael."

He indicated the nearby sofa. "You've been out walking? Then you'll need a drink." He beckoned to a nearby waiter. "What will you have? Coke? Lemonade? You need something."

"Bottled water, please."

He waited while she drank, looking her over. Had she changed so much? Her blond hair was shorter, she knew that, and her nose already pink from her afternoon in the sun. Was he noticing that she too had gained a little weight? She pulled her camera bag closer beside her on the sofa. This was ten times harder than she'd thought it would be.

"So," he said. "No one's told me what you're doing in Singapore."

"I'm on assignment, of course."

"I guessed that much. What is it this time?"

"I'm working on a book with nine other photographers, or I will be in two weeks. We'll each live with a different family for seven days and photograph them."

"In two weeks? And you're here already?"

"Getting good pictures takes more than point and click, you know. I usually come early to get a feel for a place."

"Especially since you've never worked here before." When her silence confirmed the statement, he tipped his head. "I've often wondered why. You've worked plenty of places around here."

"Why, Michael." She gave him a restrained smile. "You've been following my work."

He shrugged. "So, Tessa? Why now? Nothing better?"

She smoothed her dress down over her knees. "The job attracted me."

"Oh?"

He obviously expected more.

"I'm not an angry reformer, you know, out to change the world. I never was. Open graves in Chechnya, the horrors in Rwanda—" She shook her head vehemently. "But this job—this appeals to me. Real life, nothing extraordinary, just people living and coping, showing in everyday ways who they really are."

"But even so, a challenge to catch on film."

She lifted her chin. "I can do it."

He responded by raising his eyebrows. "I'm sure you can."

Too late she realized how defensive her response must have sounded. She took a deep breath and tried to relax. "Tell me about Singapore. You've been here two years, haven't you?"

"Over three and a half." He seemed almost bored by the fact.

She cleared her throat and tried again. "It's as clean as the travel books say, but a little strange as well, don't you think?"

"Strange?" He frowned. "If by strange you mean Singapore's many rules, it's all true. No spitting, no jaywalking—"

"And video cameras in public restrooms to make sure everyone flushes? Do they really do that?"

"No. That's just a rumor." He grinned, a little of the old Michael showing through, and pointed a thumb toward the women's room. "In a hotel like this they take care of the problem with automatic flushing."

"Why do people put up with it—the rules, I mean, and the fines?"

"That's easy. A well-behaved, law-abiding labor force attracts foreign money. Look around you. Singapore has assumed a major economic role in this area of the world."

"So everything comes back to money." She managed a laugh. "Spoken like a true banker, Michael."

He smiled, not bothering to deny it, then glanced at his watch.

"Someplace you have to be, Michael?"

"Yes, actually, I'm supposed to meet some people at five-thirty". He gave her a speculative glance. "You're welcome to come if you'd like. It's just a few friends, a last send-off for someone going back to the States."

She jumped up. "But I'll change first."

He rose as well. "Don't bother. You'll be a welcome relief from business suits."

She hesitated. Should she be pleased that he liked the dress or offended that he could think she would go looking this wilted? "I need to stash my gear anyway."

"Leave your cameras behind?" Humor glimmered again in his blue eyes. "I didn't realize you could stand up straight without at least one of them hanging off your shoulder."

She grinned. "If I start to wobble, will you catch me?"

"Now there's a thought." And then came the smile she remembered best, the one that reached his eyes and infused his whole face with warmth and humor and undeniable charm. "Any time, Tessa. You know that."

"I—" She pointed a finger toward the upper floors. "I'll just be a minute."

Alone in the elevator, after leaving her gear in the hotel safe, she pressed her cheek against the cool steel wall. Four years of relentlessly trying to forget, and it was still the same—the effect of that smile. Ridiculous the way it made her feel. She had to pull herself together again before going down.

She changed her sundress for a loose-fitting blue rayon dress with a higher neckline and added fresh makeup. But no blusher. Her cheeks had enough color already.

"Michael?"

He snapped his briefcase shut and stood. Taking in her change of clothes, he smiled his approval. "You look great. Now let's get going."

Outside, the air settled down like a weighted robe on her

shoulders. He looked up at the sky, still sunny and clear. "Checking for rain," he said. "It comes at a moment's notice, especially in January."

She nodded. "In fact, I've heard you can tell who's lived here longest by how quickly people get their umbrellas up." She took in his suit pants and briefcase and apparently empty pockets. "And yet you don't even carry one. Living dangerously, Michael?"

He tipped his head, humor apparent again. "Would that surprise you?"

She grinned. "Ha—you probably have one tucked neatly away in your briefcase." Wiping moisture from her forehead, she added, "As humid as this air is, an umbrella would be superfluous anyway. I'll end up drenched one way or another."

"Just as well I decided against the MRT and called a taxi, then. We're headed to Harry's on Boat Quay."

He took a few steps toward the street level, but she stopped where she was, making him look back up at her.

"Are you saying if I weren't with you, Michael, you'd actually take mass transit? I can hardly believe that."

"Why not?"

"Your time's too valuable, of course."

He laughed. "Fair comment. I do usually hire a taxi. But all else being equal, I knew you'd prefer riding the MRT."

She longed to tease him more—such gallantry, to descend to the hurried, workaday world of the Mass Rapid Transit for her sake—but followed him meekly into the taxi instead. She wasn't really interested in flirting.

"Where are you coming from," he said, once they were seated, "to find this heat so bad?"

"Kazakhstan." She leaned forward. Countless small posters were pasted to the front seat, notice after notice overlapping each other, explaining fares and surcharges and call bookings and more. The government had provided a few: *Make Courtesy Our Way of Life; Don't Spit; Speak Mandarin.*

"Take note of this one." Michael tapped a handwritten sign near the top: *Ask for plastic bag if you are likely to vomit.* Tessa met his smile with one of her own.

The driver, identified as a Mr. Lim Fang Peng, glanced back at a corner. "You in Singapore long?"

"My friend is visiting," Michael said.

"You want I drive around, show you sights? Or not?"

"Not tonight, thank you. We're a little late as it is."

"Okay lah. I hurry."

Michael and Tessa exchanged glances. Without wings, there wasn't much chance of speed along Orchard Road. She settled back against the seat.

"Tell me about Kazakhstan," Michael said. "Were you there long?"

She was never anywhere long—had he forgotten that? Or was the question, so blandly stated, designed to needle her? She rubbed a hand over her forehead. That couldn't be right. This was what came of parting as they had. So many good memories lost, so much trust.

"Tessa?"

"I had a couple jobs in Kazakhstan, the most important being photos for a natural gas company's annual report. They wanted to give investors a more personal view of what their money was doing. I stayed a few extra days and did a spread for a missions magazine and some other personal work." She hesitated. "I do use my photography, you know, as much as I can, to further God's cause in the world."

"Yes. I remember you saying that."

Did he? She had never been sure, afterwards, that he'd

15

heard *anything* she said that last horrible day in Seoul.

She lifted her eyes to his and thought she saw a little of her own bleakness mirrored in his own. But no. When he spoke, he sounded as calm as ever.

"Singapore must make for quite a change from Kazakhstan. How do you keep it all straight, having the right clothes, I mean?"

"I store my work in Illinois at my father's house. I get back there every two or three months. But I keep a lot of my things in Japan, too, with my mother."

"Ah."

"That's where I came from this morning, though I was only there a couple of days."

"I see your mother occasionally, and Charles, too, of course."

"Yes. She told me they had dinner with you before Christmas."

That topic used up, they both fell silent. Within moments, the taxi turned a corner and crossed a short white bridge.

"Boat Quay," Michael said. "We'll get out here, please," he told the driver.

Before them, the sidewalk curved along the river into a wide promenade dotted with palms and benches and lined with Victorian shophouses in pastel shades. Newly restored and converted into bars and restaurants, the shophouses spilled tables and chairs out onto the esplanade, bringing with them strains of live music and the tantalizing fragrance of food.

She drew back against the railing, wondering how much of the scene she could fit into a picture, then decided her best shot would be in the morning. From across the river, perhaps, with the palm fronds that lined that side in silhouette. The sun would illuminate the turquoise, cream, and apricot on the buildings, casting shimmering reflections into the water, and the gleaming skyscrapers in the background would provide a sharp contrast to the quaint foreground buildings. An added bonus, the Chinese characters spread across the shophouses would help identify the location.

She longed to see what the picture would look like. The bridge was there; it would take only a minute to run across....

"This way," Michael said, a little abruptly.

She looked at him. He must have seen what she was doing. Was he upset, irritated perhaps, because she was setting up a shot? Some things obviously never changed.

Mark it down, she told herself. *This is why it all fell through four years ago.*

She pushed past him, walking quickly enough in the direction he pointed to put some distance between them.

He called her name from behind, and she stopped, tried for a smile, and turned to face him. He was frowning.

"Something the matter?" he said.

"Of course not. What could be wrong?"

He nodded, but continued to frown, and she almost panicked. After all this time, still so much between them. Would she *never* get past this? She shook the thought away and cleared her throat. "I'm fine, Michael."

"Good. Then here we are."

He pointed across the stone walkway to the last shophouse. Crowds of people stood in groups outside the bar, talking and laughing over glasses of beer.

She took a deep breath and stepped into the noisy hum of Harry's Quayside Bar.

TWO

Michael led her to a high round table in the corner. Six people sat at the wicker chairs and stools—three women, one of them Asian, and three men, all of European background. One of the women spoke Michael's name, and everyone at the table turned to look at them.

And then oddly—too quickly—the man across the table sat back, turned his face aside and then down. He frowned, as if seeing something on the floor, then slipped off his stool, out of sight.

Michael didn't seem to notice, but in the one glimpse Tessa had before the man disappeared from view, she had seen an immediate and profound animosity on his face. Directed at her?

"Michael, you dog." The man on this side of the table stood to greet them. "Here we were wondering where you had gotten off to, and you show up with company. Where did you find this lovely lady?"

"Gus Dolan," Michael told Tessa. "Gus occasionally does what we call work at SIMEX, the Singapore International Monetary Exchange—"

"I object," Gus said. "I *rarely* do what you call work."

"The rest of us are at Chadsworth Bank—Violet Wong and Nigel Hawthorne, Jillian Thomas, Sondra Howell, and next to her Blake Hoffman."

The brown-haired man had sat up again, but now he held the tips of his fingers against his forehead, effectively blocking off her view of his face.

She frowned. Blake Hoffman. The name didn't sound familiar. How strange.

Michael smiled at the woman across the table. "Sondra is the one leaving us—"

"Deserting us, you mean," Jillian said. "And to get married, of all things." She swung her shoulder-length brown hair woefully from side to side. "How could you do it, Sondra?"

Gus began humming a dirge, and everyone except Nigel lifted their glasses in a mournful salute.

"It's not that bad," Nigel said. His accent was English, and although the others appeared to be in their early thirties, Nigel was closer to forty. "I happen to like being married."

Sondra laughed. "The rest of you guys are just jealous."

Michael put a hand on Tessa's shoulder. "Everyone, this is Tessa Brooks."

Gus pulled a chair over from a nearby table. "Sit here beside me, Tessa Brooks."

The empty chair now stood between Gus and Blake. This should be interesting. But as soon as she sat down, Blake turned toward Sondra, on his other side, exposing to Tessa little more than his left arm and shoulder.

A very cold shoulder.

Michael pulled another chair to the space beside Jillian and motioned for a waitress.

"Coke for me," Tessa said. "With lots of ice."

Gus leaned an expansive arm across the back of Tessa's chair. His wide, friendly smile revealed gleaming white teeth, and a twinkle shone in his eyes. "What a beautiful woman you have brought us, Michael. Where did you find her?"

"Tessa is my step-cousin," Michael said. "Her mother married my uncle."

"And you're visiting Michael?" Jillian said. She had a hand

now on Michael's arm. "Is that why you came to Singapore?"

"I'm a photographer," Tessa answered. "I'm here on assignment."

Sondra leaned forward past Blake, so she could see Tessa better. "What kind of photography?"

"Tessa's had work published in *Life* and *Time*," Michael said, "and many of the big travel magazines."

Tessa blinked. Four years ago he had accused her of chasing glamour. He seemed quick now to brag about her accomplishments.

Gus leaned closer. "Done any bridges lately?"

Tessa knew what was coming. "Why bridges?"

"Hey, this isn't Madison County, and I'm no bored housewife, but if you'd like a guide…or anything else, I'm available."

"Thank you very much. I'll keep that in mind."

"Don't be silly," Jillian purred. "Tessa has Michael to show her around, doesn't she, Michael?"

"Of course. I'm at her disposal."

The young Chinese woman, Violet, asked about other places Tessa had worked. Her answer turned the conversation to travel in general and their own weekend jaunts in particular.

Under cover of the bar's lowered lights, Tessa watched Michael. The expatriate life in Singapore apparently offered plenty of time for travel, mostly to resorts in nearby Bali and Kuala Lumpur. Michael added his own comments—usually wry—to the discussion. What intrigued Tessa most was Jillian's response to him. At one point, she put a hand on Michael's arm again. Was she emphasizing her claim to Michael? He didn't seem abnormally attentive to her, and yet he had chosen to pull his chair next to hers.

As if aware of her scrutiny, Michael turned. Their gazes met and held.

She pushed her chair back so quickly it almost fell. "Please excuse me for a minute."

"Me, too," Jillian said and followed Tessa to the bathroom. She propped herself against a nearby wall and grinned. "Are you ever a surprise!"

Tessa pulled out a comb and ran it through her hair. "Michael doesn't usually show up with a date?"

"Though you're not really a date, are you—being related I mean?"

Tessa didn't bother answering, just opened her compact and applied herself to the havoc caused by Singapore's high humidity.

Jillian disappeared into a stall. When she came out, her voice had lost its seductive drawl. "I was wondering, just how long are you planning to be in Singapore?"

"A month, probably."

"Where are you staying?"

"My publisher booked a room at the Hyatt Regency, off Orchard Road. The first night's complimentary. I'll move to the YMCA tomorrow, or someplace even cheaper if I can find it."

"Yeah?" Jillian shook off her wet hands. "Cheaper, huh?"

"I get a set fee for most assignments, but I have to pay my own living expenses."

"Hmm. Well, if you're serious, I'll rent you a room in my apartment. I could do with the extra money, and the price will be much less than the Hyatt Regency—say forty dollars a night?"

Tessa's lipstick paused midstroke. "You mean it?"

Jillian talked fast, like a salesman with one foot in the door: "The apartment's intended for one person and only has one bathroom, and the room I can give you isn't much better than an office, though I do have a bed in there. But you'd have kitchen privileges, which you wouldn't have at the YMCA."

"How's the security for your apartment building?"

"Security? Why?"

"My gear. It's expensive and easy to fence."

"You mean like cameras and stuff. Sure. There's a security guard downstairs that we have to check in with, and there's a dead bolt on my door and an extra lock on the French windows leading onto the balcony. Other than that, I don't have any place with a lock inside the apartment. Sorry."

"That sounds like enough," Tessa said. "Give me your number. I'll think about it."

"Better yet, come over for lunch tomorrow, say, one o'clock? I'll pick up some Chinese, or Indian, or anything you want. You can see the place before you decide." Jillian smiled, an open, friendly smile. "Please come."

Definitely much nicer without a man around, Tessa decided. "Okay. I'll be there."

As they emerged from the alcove with the restrooms, Tessa caught Blake Hoffman watching for her from across the room. Stranger and stranger. He broke the contact almost immediately, but not before she'd gotten a good look at him. He had pleasant features. Quite unremarkable, in fact…except for the disgust in his eyes.

Disgust or spite.

She returned to her seat beside him. It didn't make sense. He seemed easygoing enough with the rest of them, quite affable in fact. He laughed at the right times, ordered a refill for Sondra, and received as many greetings from passing colleagues as anyone else at the table. Judging from the smiles he drew from Violet and Sondra, Blake Hoffman knew how to charm a woman.

What had Tessa done to earn his disfavor?

She touched his arm, and he leaned his head in her general direction.

"Have you been in Singapore long?" she said.

"Only a few months." His accent stood out, a softly edged Southern accent, not from the deep south, but definitely mellow. She wanted to ask him where he came from exactly—she liked tracing accents—but he shifted his attention immediately toward Michael, making it difficult again for Tessa to see his face. "A *good* few months, wouldn't you say?"

"Absolutely," Michael said. "It's been a while since we've seen such fast success."

Jillian, sitting across from Tessa, rolled her eyes. However well Blake managed to charm everyone else, Jillian wasn't impressed.

"Blake's the newest superstar at Chadsworth," Gus whispered to Tessa. "He's making big loans every week. Poor Jillian thinks he's upstaging her."

Michael stood and lifted his glass. "To you, Sondra, and your future happiness. We'll miss you greatly. Here's a small token of our good wishes for your future and the happiness of your marriage."

He handed her an envelope from his inner pocket, and everyone stood to join the toast. More good wishes and cheers followed, Gus called for a taxi, and the party moved outside. They stood around talking until the taxi arrived.

"I'm off to home," Nigel said. "Have a good weekend, everyone."

"He'll take the MRT," Michael explained. "The station's close."

Everyone else began piling into the taxi. "We're going over to the Warehouse for dancing," Gus said. "Sure you don't want to come?"

Michael shook his head. "No, go on. We'll be fine."

Jillian leaned out the backseat window. "Don't forget, Tessa.

23

Tomorrow. I'll be expecting you at one."

The taxi pulled away. "You could have gone," Tessa said.

"Not my kind of party. Gus knew that."

He had his hands in his pockets, his face turned upriver. The evening sun, lower toward the horizon, was full on his face, perfect for highlighting the smooth lines of his forehead and jaw and the firm strength of his mouth. She reached for her camera.

He caught the movement and flashed his smile again. "Starting to wobble, Tessa?"

"It's the horizontal lighting." She held up her hands to frame the shot. "It would flatter even a face like yours."

"What a shame to miss it then."

She scrunched her nose at him. As if, with Jillian around, he didn't know how attractive he was. "What now? Are you taking me to dinner?"

"If you'd like. Where shall we go?"

Neon lights glowed along the river. The music and the crowds had grown. It seemed every restaurant was full, with more people coming all the time.

"No fair," she said. "I hear eating out is the national pastime in Singapore. How could I make a choice?"

"There's a perfectly good hawker center nearby where you can have your pick of all the best Singapore offers—Indian, Malay, Chinese, and much more. Enough variety even for you, Tessa."

"And cheap, too, so I've heard, so we'll save that for when I'm buying. Tonight take me to your favorite place, Michael." She slanted a grin at him. "I know you have one."

"But *only* one?"

"Absolutely." In fact, she was counting on it. Now, more than ever, seeing him standing there, knowing he wasn't for her, knowing she had to come to terms with that, she wanted to be reminded why. "And you'll even order the same thing—I'm sure of it. The same table if you can get it."

"People *can* change, Tessa."

Quiet words, spoken with conviction. They seemed to boom through her mind. Someone bumped her from behind, and she heard their apology as if through a tunnel, but she couldn't move, couldn't speak. His eyes, so blue, so intense, met and held hers, and she felt an ineffable sadness creeping over her. Of course people could change. Hadn't they proved for themselves how fickle emotions could be?

He touched her arm. "Come along, then," he said. "I might surprise you—starting with the MRT." He grinned. "It's easier than a taxi this time of night."

An hour later, her fingers smeared with sauce from a plate of Dan Ryan's baby back ribs, Tessa had to admit he was right. He had surprised her. She had expected soft music, linen tablecloths, a thick steak and a perfectly baked potato. Instead, here was Michael, a big napkin tucked into his collar, looking quite comfortable in the noisy atmosphere around them.

Not that his fingers had any sauce on them or his chin a smidgen of grease. Oh, no. Michael would insist on using a knife and fork. Such neat hands, nails trimmed, skin smooth. And such very white cuffs.

"Not completely a surprise," she said. "You did choose American food."

"Believe me," he said, after he had wiped his mouth, "you'll have plenty of opportunities to enjoy Singapore's spicy flavors over the next few weeks. I thought tonight, coming from Kazakhstan, you wouldn't mind a little taste of home."

She smiled. "And this is delicious in any city. Thank you."

"I'm glad you like it. Now about this project. I assume the government's funding it?"

"Perhaps." She shook her head. "I don't know. I'm being paid by a local publishing company—Asia Premier Publications."

He glanced around the area where they were sitting. No one seemed to be listening, but even so he spoke in a softer voice. "It sounds like something the government would do—choose model families, show them to advantage, publish them in a flashy, upscale package—"

"Why? Why would they do that?"

His lips twisted into an ironic smile. "Believe it or not, to encourage women to marry and settle down."

Tessa almost dropped the rib she was holding.

He wasn't finished. "Most women in Singapore delay marriage, especially professional women, and according to a recent survey one woman in four says she'll never marry at all."

Her jaw stiffened. "It is their choice, isn't it? They still have that freedom here?"

"It's a choice the government wants to change." He wiped his hands on his napkin, then pulled his cuffs further down over his wrists. "The PAP—that's the ruling party—wants women to have children, especially the brightest, most accomplished women, so they can increase that portion of the gene pool."

"You're kidding—'the most accomplished'? You'd think they'd want them to keep working, to make use of their talents and skills."

"Oh, they do. They're willing to provide whatever day care is necessary to keep these women on the job, and other incentives as well—better housing, better schools." He gave a brief smile. "They even sponsor a matchmaking service. In spite of all that, it's still primarily the lower-class, less educated women who want children."

Tessa pressed her lips together. They were having two conversations, she thought, and only one of them was about Singaporean women. She managed to contain herself with an effort. "And you think this book on families is just another ploy to get what they want?"

"Not a ploy," Michael said. "A campaign. That's what the government calls these things. You saw a sample on the back of the taxi seat. And yes, I do. I'll prove it to you. This family, the one you're photographing, the husband and wife are both professionals?"

"No, they aren't. Mr. Soon works on an orchid farm."

"His wife?"

"She is a teacher."

"And children? They do have children?"

"Three. A girl and two boys."

"Perfect for the purpose of highlighting an educated woman, wouldn't you agree?"

"Not exactly. There's also a niece living with them, and a brother in his twenties, and Mr. Soon's widowed mother."

"Even so, lots of opportunity to show how she can have it all—family, money, job, success."

Tessa wasn't sure she liked the idea of being part of a carefully orchestrated government campaign, especially one like this, but perhaps given the political realities in Singapore, she couldn't expect anything else. "You sound very cynical."

He smiled a little ruefully. "Don't worry, Tessa. Compared to some of the tactics the government uses, a photo essay is pretty mild. It looks like you're finished. Ready to go?"

Outside, the air was balmy, and the spirits of the people

around them even more festive in the glittering city lights.

"Shall we walk?" Michael said. "The hotel's only a few blocks away."

"Please."

But within a few hundred feet, he paused. "What did Jillian mean when she mentioned seeing you tomorrow?"

"She offered to share her flat with me during the next month."

"Really? The bank provides her housing, you know."

"Could she get in trouble, renting a room to me?"

"Borderline. I doubt she'll let anyone know you're paying."

"How much does her apartment cost, do you know?"

"Thirty thousand U.S. a year."

Tessa's mouth gaped. "To rent it?"

"There are plenty that cost more, believe me, priced for expatriate companies to pay for."

He waited for her to speak again, but she was too busy calculating Jillian's fee to respond. Forty dollars a night worked out pretty close to half. Perhaps she wasn't Jillian's first boarder.

"Do you think you'll take the room?" he said.

"It would save a lot of money."

"True." He shrugged and began walking again.

She scurried to catch up with him. "Michael, what's the matter?"

"Isn't this pretty sudden?"

She smiled. "I'm only here a few weeks, Michael, five or six at the most. I don't have time to check out her résumé."

"You might wish you had with Jillian."

"You tell me—what should I know about her?"

"I wouldn't recommend living with her, for one."

"Why not?"

At the tone of her voice, he turned to look at her. His features grew still.

"Michael?"

"Do what you want, Tessa—which in this case will probably be fine. Jillian is an intelligent, hard-working woman, who knows Singapore well. You'll learn a lot living with her."

About Singapore…or about Michael?

"That's not much help," she said.

"I shouldn't advise you, Tessa, one way or the other."

She pressed her lips together. She knew what he was thinking, so sure of himself. She should take his advice, refuse Jillian's offer, and all without a word of explanation from him.

This time she was the one who set off walking.

How little he had changed, everything still black and white—his way right and everything else wrong. And that conversation in the restaurant. He was as determined as ever to fault her motives.

They walked the few remaining blocks to her hotel in silence, and at the entryway, she stopped him from going inside. "I'll be fine from here, thank you, Michael."

His body was very close beside her, so close she could easily have touched the cotton of his still-spotless shirt.

"Tessa—" His hand came up, and he almost gripped her arm—almost. She felt his thumb brush against her, but his fist closed over air instead, and he stepped back abruptly. "Of course. I'll call you tomorrow."

She glanced back from inside. He stood where she'd left him, staring down at the sidewalk, arms crossed, wearing a frown.

Upstairs she flung herself backwards onto the bed and for long moments gave in to weariness. What a day, hard for them both, and yet he had said he would call tomorrow.

Perhaps he had something to prove as well.

Michael stood a moment outside the hotel, then turned west on Orchard Road, away from the direction of his apartment on Ardmore Park.

She was here, finally. Impatient to see her, he'd ended his three o'clock appointment early, only to arrive at her hotel to find her gone. He had stared at the same page for thirty minutes, read the same paragraph three times, and had finally given up. And then there she was, so much still Tessa—the same glow, the same intelligence, the same spark and brightness. In her green dress she had looked both energetic and driven, and if anything more competent than ever. Yet her smile, barely visible under tucked head, had tugged painfully at his heart.

It hurt to see her so guarded with him, edgy and defensive, but he had expected that. Of course he had. He even knew her reasons.

He walked on down Orchard Road, unaware of how far he was going.

How strange life was. Growing up, he'd envisioned himself falling in love with a woman he could protect and nourish. Instead, in the space of one month four years ago, he'd fallen completely and irrevocably in love with Tessa Brooks, self-sufficient and free-spirited, a woman who needed capturing, not protecting.

He'd proposed marriage, but even as he was closing his grip on her, she'd been offered her first big assignment. Like a butterfly she had flown away—so close and then gone. Another assignment and then another. Six months later, frustrated and angry, he'd broken off the relationship.

In the years since, determined to put her behind him, he had repeatedly found himself sitting across the table from her mother, hoping for news of her. And while he hadn't exactly been losing sleep over her—at least not since the early months—he nevertheless kept a running and complete collection of her published work, a collection that at first surprised and then shamed him with its power and beauty. He'd had no business expecting her to abandon photography for him. It would have been like pinning a butterfly and putting it under glass.

Yet having her close to him, inches, touching distance, he'd felt the old desperation wash over him again, the desire to grip and control, to somehow own the life that was Tessa. He badly wanted her in his life.

He stopped in his tracks and cast his gaze up past the lights and the trees, past the skyscrapers and the stars to the distant darkness of the sky. *If this is a second chance, let me do it right, please.*

No coercion this time. No rebuke or criticism. He wanted the real Tessa, free and unfettered, full of spirit and joy. This time he would win more than her consent.

This time he would win her heart.

He relaxed, relieved to have the decision made, and looked around. He was almost to Dhoby Ghaut at the far western end of Orchard Road, far enough that he'd be taking the MRT home. How had he gotten here?

He grinned. He'd always found her extremely distracting.

THREE

Tessa slept in the next morning. After a long, luxurious shower, she sat for a moment on her bed and considered her options. Then she packed up her belongings and checked out. If it didn't work with Jillian, she would find a cheaper hotel. She arrived at Jillian's apartment, fourth floor up, with her big duffel bag, her carry-on bag, and the custom-made wooden crate she used for shipping strobe equipment.

"Whoa," Jillian said when Tessa opened the apartment door. "This must mean you've decided to move in."

"I hope so. But if not, I'll still be glad to leave the Hyatt Regency's prices behind." Tessa looked around. The living area was small, with nondescript windows, plain furniture, and nothing to break the bland color scheme. But it did have blessedly cool air. "Thank goodness you have air conditioning. This heat would be murder on my cameras."

"Honey, it wouldn't be any good for my health, either. I'm no masochist."

Jillian had pulled her shoulder-length brown hair up into a pony tail, but had done a sloppy job of it, with strands hanging down her neck in the back. Her clothes were as nondescript as the room—faded blue shorts and an olive green shirt that said "GET A LIFE" across the chest. The alluring woman from Harry's had disappeared, though Tessa suspected that a man in the vicinity—any man—would bring her back again.

"Come on," Jillian said. "I'll show you around. I have the two bedrooms—you'd have this one back here. The furniture comes with the place, it's horrible, isn't it? The kitchen's okay, though I rarely cook myself—there's a great deli nearby—and that's about it, except for the balcony, of course, not that I ever go out there. What do you think? You wouldn't believe how much it costs for such a small space—but I told you, didn't I? You'd be paying exactly half the rent. I'm not charging any extra for the short-term lease, I promise. I sure hope you'll take it."

Tessa nodded. "It looks fine." Considering what Michael said about the bank paying the rent, Tessa's contribution would be a nice bonus for Jillian. Even so, the price would be far beneath a comparable hotel.

"How long will you be staying?" Jillian said.

"Three weeks at least. After that I have a job in India for a week and another in Australia for two weeks. I might keep the room through those, but I'll leave for sure after that."

"So six weeks in all."

"Will that work?"

"Sure."

Tessa retrieved her wallet from the photo bag on top of her pile. "How about VISA?"

Jillian looked surprised, and Tessa laughed. "Just kidding. I picked up cash on the way over."

"I'm impressed. When you said yesterday you needed to think about it, I thought, she's just like Michael, this'll take her a week to decide—"

"No—"

"But I should have known better, of course. How cautious can you be, dashing all over the globe like you do?"

Tessa shook her head. "Michael and I aren't at all the same. You'll see. Shall I take this stuff into my room?"

"I'll help." Jillian picked up the duffel bag and let loose an expressive word. "What's in here—weights?"

"Photo gear. That one has tripods and lightstands, with

most of my clothes as packing. I'll take it."

"You must work up quite an appetite lugging that load around," Jillian said, when they finished moving the gear. "I bought Indonesian for lunch. There's a place nearby that does a great *rendang*—this one's beef and plenty spicy, but I also bought some chicken *satay*, which is milder, and a few noodle dishes, which should be safe. And there's beer or Coke, whichever you want."

Tessa breathed in the snappy scents. "This looks great." She pushed some noodles onto her plate and added several skewers of chicken and a portion of the beef dish. Cooked in coconut milk, the *rendang* was as fiery hot as Jillian had said, but Tessa loved it. "Wow, water, I think, if I can get some ice."

"Help yourself, in the freezer." Jillian washed a mouthful down with a swallow of beer. "Now, come on—about Michael. How long have you known him?"

"You probably know him better than I do."

"You're kidding—no one knows Michael well. I'm convinced of it. Which makes him all the more interesting, don't you think?"

"I suppose."

"Come on, give," Jillian said. "All your life?"

"No. I first met him ten years ago when I was eighteen. I was spending a month in Japan with my mother and Charles—that's my stepfather, Michael's uncle. I had just graduated from high school, and Michael from college. He appeared during the last few days of my visit."

"So you're like…brother and sister?"

A bite of chicken lodged in Tessa's throat, and she reached for her water.

"You could have stayed with him," Jillian continued. "And for nothing, too. He has an extra bedroom."

"No. We're not close like that." Tessa pulled the third dish on the table toward her. "What did you say the name of this salad was?"

"*Gado-Gado*. It has a coconut-peanut dressing. They go in big for peanuts and coconut down in Indonesia."

"But what a treat to have such wonderful food available. I'm not surprised you don't bother cooking."

"No need to get bored in Singapore—at least not where food's concerned." Jillian pushed her own plate away and took another drink of beer. "Now, tell me about being a photographer. Why do you like it?"

"Maybe because every day is different."

"You sure move around a lot."

"But it's more than the travel. Like in Thailand. I was there on a shoot for a United Nations project. I stayed with a family for three weeks. One day, after the first really hard rain of the monsoons, they took me outside and showed me how to catch *maeng man* ants. That's not an opportunity everybody gets."

"What on earth did you want them for?"

"To eat them, of course. They tasted pretty good fried—crunchy, like potato chips."

Jillian's jaw dropped.

"The trick was to grab the adult ants just as they came out of the burrows, before they flew away, then shake off the baby ants they were carrying—the babies have a vicious sting—and pop the adults into a bottle."

"And I was afraid you wouldn't want to eat the *rendang*."

Tessa grinned.

Jillian's eyes narrowed. "So I guess it doesn't run in the family—this religious thing Michael has."

"What do you mean?"

"It's a big thing with him, you know, his Christianity."

Tessa shook her head. "Why would you think it wasn't with me?"

"Oh." Jillian blinked, considering. "Maybe because you're so unconventional. I mean—ants, as a snack. And you did say you were different from Michael."

"I am a Christian—and if it's my job that surprises you, that I can wander around doing strange things, there's plenty of room in God's kingdom for people like me. I think he likes what I do. In fact, that's why I do it."

"Weird." Jillian scrunched her nose up. "Michael does that, too, you know, talking about God as if he really knows him. Not often, I mean, just now and then, but ugh—" She shuddered, then stood and began gathering up the empty containers. "Why would you want a god hanging over your shoulder all the time, watching what you do?"

"Friends do that, Jillian. Family does. They watch out for you. Why not God?"

Jillian lowered the stack of carry-out packages to the table. "But this friend, as you call him, has got all these rules, and if you mess up, well—" She waved her hand toward the bank of windows at the end of the room. "Trust me. This is Singapore. People here do the most bizarre things to keep their gods from savaging them. I'd rather live my own life, thank you, the way I want to, without anyone telling me what's right and what's wrong."

She smashed the cartons together and shoved her way into the kitchen. In a minute, she was back, stalking toward her bedroom.

"Wait, Jillian. It's okay."

Jillian paused, stared at Tessa, then shrugged. "I'm going shopping. Come if you want to. I have to change." She turned and disappeared into her bedroom.

Tessa sat looking after her, stunned. She knew a little about what Jillian meant. In Singapore, during the Hindu festival of Thaipusam, people pierced their bodies with dozens of skewers so they could balance sixty-pound platforms on them, and then walked five miles under the hot sun through cheering crowds. The ritual, outlawed in India because it was so inhumane, was thought to earn an extra measure of benevolence not only for the young men who endured the ordeal but for their families as well.

Tessa sighed. Jillian didn't understand much, if she equated what Jesus offered with a ritual like that.

It's in your hands, she whispered. *Show her the truth, please.*

Michael hadn't called the hotel during the morning, and if he called the Hyatt Regency now he'd miss her. Tessa found Jillian's phone book and looked up his name, pausing when she saw it printed on the page. Michael Lawton. She ran her finger over the letters. There had been a time, before things fell apart between them, when she had talked to him almost every night, even when it meant calling him long distance. Now she didn't even know his number.

"Who are you calling?" Jillian said from the doorway of her bedroom. "If it's Michael, he's probably at Chadsworth. The number's on speed dial."

He answered on the first ring.

"I'm at Jillian's," Tessa said. "I thought you might want to know. I've decided to accept her offer."

"I see."

"You did say you were going to call. I thought you might have missed me at the Hyatt."

"Yes. About church. Would you like to go with me tomorrow?"

"What kind of church do you go to?"

Silence for a moment. "A Christian one?" he said.

"Funny. I meant Baptist, Methodist, American, Tamil, Chinese—what kind?"

He named the same denomination he attended in the States.

She might have known. "Okay. That's fine. What time?"

They arranged when and where to meet, and then Michael asked about her plans for the rest of the day.

"I'm going shopping with Jillian this afternoon. And tonight I'm having dinner with some people from the publishing company—editors and assistants and so forth. So thank you. I'm set."

"Good. But before you hang up, Blake says he has some files Jillian should pick up."

Tessa carried the wireless phone to the door of Jillian's room. "For you," she said.

Jillian listened for a moment, hung up the phone, and swore. "I'd sure like to know what Blake Hoffman does with his time. He's constantly shuffling work over to me." She picked up her eyeliner again. "We'll have to stop off at Chadsworth before shopping."

"Tell me about Blake Hoffman."

"What's to tell? He's a jerk. I'm surprised he doesn't shed pieces of sheep's clothing everywhere he goes." She unscrewed a tube of mascara, then paused. "No, he's not a wolf. More a snake, who sheds his entire skin at will. Someone with power comes along, something he wants, he gives them that big smile, those smooth words, but the second he sees his chance, in he goes for the kill. Ooh! He gives me the creeps."

"No kidding."

"Why'd you ask about him?"

"Because I got the impression at the bar last night that he really, really doesn't like me."

"Yeah? Well, drop a hint to Michael, will you? Everyone thinks I'm just jealous, Michael included, but that guy has undercut me more than once, taking credit for work I've done, and always in a way I couldn't prove what he was doing." She jerked the mascara away from her lashes. "Now look what I've done. Just thinking about that turkey messes me up."

"What is it you do in your job, anyway?" Tessa said.

"You mean besides doing Blake's work for him?" Jillian swiped at the smudge and started on the mascara again. "I arrange loans, same as Michael and Blake and Nigel. Nigel and I do local ones—mostly trade. It's Singapore's major industry. Michael does bigger packages for projects around the entire region—Thailand, Malaysia, Singapore."

"Projects?"

"Ship-building and construction, chemical companies—operations that big. He has to figure out how to balance their assets and ability to pay with our profit margin, so that everyone wins." Jillian stepped back from the mirror for a final review. "Okay, that's that." In slim-fitting black slacks and a cropped turquoise tee, her allure was back in force. "I'm ready."

She waited while Tessa grabbed her backpack full of photo gear, then continued her explanation in the elevator. "As for Blake, who knows? If he's not stealing someone else's work, he's off negotiating deals on his own. In the process, he's making me look bad—three million dollars worth of loans in a little over two months. With that record, he's on the fast track to becoming a projects manager, like Michael, who's on his way even higher. He's being promoted, you know, heading back to the New York office in July or August."

"Michael?"

"Yup."

Tessa hadn't heard that—but there was probably a lot about Michael that her mother wasn't passing on. She pushed that thought aside. "So Blake's a good banker?"

Jillian wrinkled her nose. "Good banker, maybe, but not good otherwise. Whoa, feel that humidity." They had stepped outside. "Is the MRT okay? The station's over on Orchard, just a couple of blocks that way. Or do you want a taxi?"

"The MRT's fine. Lead the way."

Jillian began walking. "What were we talking about? That's right—now, Michael. He's in a different class. When he wants a loan to work, somehow he finds a way. Interest rate and currency swaps, defeasance deals and long-term dated forwards, he goes on and on with these things. He's tenacious, and of course the clients love him, since the labor's as much for their benefit as the bank's."

And what about Blake? Did clients love him as well? As they approached the bank, Tessa found herself growing more and more anxious to see him again, to find out if her impressions from the night before still held. She knew one thing: she wouldn't want to be left alone in a room with him, not if she had read his expression correctly.

Jillian took her to the seventeenth floor of Chadsworth Bank. Jillian and Michael worked in the merchant banking division, which meant no accounts with the public, no tellers downstairs, no checkbooks or ATMs. But standing at the doorway behind Jillian, Tessa was surprised to see how crowded the office was, with three desks besides Jillian's own. She was even more surprised to see Michael at one of them. From Jillian's glowing report, she had expected him to have his own office, possibly on the corner, with big windows and a panoramic view. He had his sleeves rolled up and papers spread across his desk, but his smile when he saw her was quick and inviting, and she found herself stepping toward him.

With an act of will, she searched out Blake instead, who sat in the far left corner. From him she received nothing except the briefest of glances before he turned to gaze into his bottom drawer. When Jillian walked over to stand beside him, blocking off Tessa's view even more, she turned back toward Michael.

He had come around to lean against the side of his desk. Without the pristine cover of shirt cuffs, his tanned forearms showed plenty of strength, and the shoulders under the thin cotton material were obviously athletic. The weight he'd gained must have been all muscle.

"Having a good day?" he said.

"It's warm. Worse than yesterday, I think."

He went to the water dispenser in the corner of the room and brought back a paper cupful. "Here. The climate takes some getting used to—plenty of fluids or you'll dehydrate."

"Come on," Jillian said. "I've got what I need—not that I want it. I don't see why you couldn't have finished these up yourself, Blake."

"So y'all could spend more time shopping?"

Jillian began to object, but Michael spoke first. "Leave it alone, Hoffman. She works hard enough."

Jillian's smile was radiant.

"Better get going," Michael said, returning her smile. "Who knows what sales you're missing?"

Jillian scrunched her nose at Michael's teasing, grabbed Tessa's arm, and headed toward the door.

In the MRT train, while Jillian studied Blake's papers, Tessa spent the time puzzling over Blake himself. Had they met before? Perhaps on location or at a photography workshop?

She stretched her neck, aware of muscles tensing in her shoulders.

She couldn't remember him, his face or his name, and she was usually good with both. Yet there had to be a reason for his immediate aversion. If not, if this was just some kind of unbalanced, irrational response on Blake's part, something pathological or disturbed—

She shook her head back and forth, trying to shake off her alarm.

Maybe she reminded him of a snide and spiteful childhood classmate. Maybe his abusive stepmother had blond hair. Or maybe she looked like an ex-girlfriend he had fantasized about—

She put a hand to her throat. Whatever it might be, she had absolutely no reason on earth to connect Blake Hoffman with axe murderers and serial killers.

None at all.

Jillian used a search-and-rescue approach to her shopping, showing an unfailing hope that somewhere in the piles of clothing, the numerous shops, the countless racks, a perfect bargain waited to be found. Tessa, who preferred to buy reliable quality, usually from L.L. Bean or Eddie Bauer, quickly retreated behind her camera.

Singapore was indeed a shoppers' paradise, with plenty of designer boutiques, but Jillian favored the smaller stores along Orchard Road for inexpensive, locally made fashions. In the space of three hours, using lightning speed in the dressing room, she found four irresistible outfits: a silk shantung halter dress that hugged her curves, a cropped linen top with drawstring pants, a short, shaped dress in bright orange knit, and a tank dress in a muted animal print. For work, Jillian wore trim, well-made business suits with skirt lengths that went to the edge of respectability. These outfits, which went right over the precipice, had to be for evening.

More revealing than the clothes Jillian decided to purchase, however, were the men's reactions to her smiles as she walked down busy Orchard Road. She definitely had what they liked in a woman. At the men's interest, Jillian's already high energy ratcheted up another notch, darkening her eyes and giving her complexion a luminescent glow. Tessa found herself feeling more and more like the homely cousin, but Jillian's humor and enthusiasm were irresistibly winsome.

"I'm so sorry you've got this dinner to go to," Jillian said as they climbed out of a taxi at her apartment. "I'd love to show you the night life around here. We could pick up some guys, do some of the bars. There's lots of music."

Not quite Tessa's favorite agenda, but she would have enjoyed the time with Jillian. "Maybe we could have lunch together sometime next week."

"Good idea. Let's do it."

FOUR

Michael waited outside his church the next morning, under the overhang to avoid the sudden driving rain, and wondered if perhaps the storm had delayed Tessa. He glanced at his watch. No, he had come early again. He shook his head in mock dismay.

A taxi drew up, and an umbrella emerged from the back seat, followed by Tessa. "Am I late?"

"Right on time. Come on in."

"My umbrella?"

"Leave it here by the door. No one will take it."

She had tucked her short blond hair behind her ears, and her pale skin, with its dusting of freckles, had only a faint tinge of makeup on the cheeks. He liked that. It made it easier to read her blush. She wore the same blue dress she'd worn Friday evening and looked as poised and capable as she had then. Given her ready smiles and friendly nature, he wasn't surprised to see the questions in people's eyes as they walked down the hall. Was she a missionary? expatriate? tourist? friend?

He knew how he'd like to introduce her, but after two short days he wondered if he would ever get the chance. A wall seemed to have grown up between them, a wall he'd have to breach if he ever wanted to succeed with her. He wasn't sure she'd let him.

In the classroom, he waited until she had pushed her carry-all safely under her chair, then said, "We're studying First Peter. The teacher's a Scripture Union missionary."

She was looking around the room. "They're not all expatriates."

"No. About half and half."

"Do you think your pastor would let me take pictures—not this week, but next Sunday maybe, or during the week at some of the church activities?"

"What for?"

The teacher stood, and Tessa shook her head. "Later."

In his introduction, Michael explained their relationship—"My uncle married her mother"—told why Tessa was in Singapore, and saw again the instant curiosity and respect that Tessa's career elicited. She was quiet during the ensuing discussion, but interested, alert to the interaction, sitting forward especially when someone from Singapore spoke out.

He was surprised, then, when Sunday school ended, that she maneuvered him out into the hall, away from the curiosity of people in the class.

"Please, give me a tour of the church," she said. "I'm so curious. Is this mixture typical for Singapore? Do most churches have both nationals and expatriates? And the building—I'd love to see the Sunday school classes, know what activities go on during the week. Will you show me?"

"Why?"

"It's for a project I'm working on."

"A project? Even at church, Tessa?"

She stuck her chin up—a gesture he remembered from four years earlier. "We all worship in our own way, Michael Lawton. I'll walk around on my own, if you won't show me."

"Calm down." But at the door of the preschool class, he was waylaid by Joseph Fu, who was attending Michael's Bible study, and further down the hallway by Gary de Vos, who wanted to check that Michael would be at the soccer game that week.

Tessa glanced at her watch. "At least introduce me to the people who do your children's church. We have time for that."

"I'm not even sure I know."

"Michael! Please."

"Husband or wife? I'm sure it's a couple that runs it."

"Whichever is less likely to give me permission to photograph their class. I'll tackle the harder first."

He took her into the fellowship hall where people were drinking coffee, asked a few questions, and led her to a middle-aged woman sitting at a table. "Martha, could I have a word with you?"

"It's...Michael, isn't it?"

"Michael Lawton. My cousin here—Tessa Brooks—is visiting Singapore. She wanted to meet you."

Curious, the woman turned to Tessa, who sat down and held out her hand. Michael couldn't see Tessa's face, standing as he was behind her, but she must have given Martha Fisher one of her big, winning smiles, because Martha's face relaxed and a smile spread across her features. Michael stepped back. Tessa could handle this on her own.

By the time he returned with two cups of coffee, Tessa was standing.

"Thank you, Martha. I'll talk to the pastor during the week, make sure it's okay, and then I'll see you next Sunday."

Michael led her away. "She said yes?"

Tessa took a quick sip of her coffee. A smile lit up her face. "You remembered, Michael. Cream, no sugar."

"Details," he said and had to clear his throat. "My head is full of them."

"And you can pull them up at will? That's a nice trait for a banker."

46

More than that. She could ask him anything—her favorite line from *The Princess Bride,* whether she liked tomatoes on her sandwiches, the tune she hummed when her mind was wandering. It was all coming back to him.

He crushed the empty cup in his hand before throwing it away. "You didn't say. Did she agree?"

"If the pastor does. It'll take a lot of work on her part, of course. I usually start with a group Polaroid. Then she or her husband will have to stay after and name all the children, so I can get signed releases from their parents."

"Do many refuse?"

"Not if I promise them pictures."

He grinned. "A genuine Tessa Brooks photograph. I wonder if they realize what they're getting."

A trace of pink tinged her cheeks. "It's time for church, don't you think? Shouldn't we go?"

Her hair had slipped from behind her ear. He lifted his hand, wanting to tuck it away, but she turned and took a step before he could touch her. He let his arm fall back into place. Patience.

After church, Tessa expected Michael to return her to Jillian's apartment. Instead he took her to lunch at the Nonya and Baba Restaurant on River Valley Road. Again he surprised her. From her research she knew that the Nonya cuisine came from the intermarriage of Chinese immigrants to Malay women. This hardly seemed the kind of food Michael would like.

"Do you eat here often?" she said.

"First time." He didn't look up, not at first, but at her continued stillness, he lowered his menu as well. "Now what are you thinking?"

"Are you saying we're here for my sake? Like traveling on the MRT, an experience I would enjoy?"

He held her gaze. He was so calm, his inner stillness rarely ruffled. "I still don't see where this is heading, Tessa."

"I just want to know. Have you ever eaten Nonya food before, or is this the first time, in all the three plus years you've been here?"

"Ah. I understand now. As it turns out, Mrs. Ling, my cleaning lady, is a Nonya. She comes in three times a week and leaves a meal for me. I'm not likely to go out for this kind of food, am I, when I have the real thing at home?"

"Oh."

He set his menu aside. "You seem to think I'm one of those smug expatriates who eats only American food, don't you? Who gets to know only American people and enjoys only American activities? Now why would you think that of me?"

Tessa lifted her menu and frowned in concentration at the selections. "Stupid of me, I suppose."

"Tessa…"

Down came the menu again. "But you did refuse to try sushi, don't you remember? And you raked me over the coals when I suggested I might sign up for a session at that Zen monastery. And I had to drag you through the Shinto shrine."

"We were late for dinner that day at the shrine. And raw fish and seaweed still don't appeal to me. As for the Zen monastery, immersing yourself to that extent in false teaching was—and is—a bad idea. You should have known better."

"Instead we're supposed to hide our heads in the sand, afraid of what's out there?"

"Three months under a Zen master? That's not a question of courage."

"I wanted to understand Oriental thinking. It would have

been like a philosophy course for me, not a religious exercise."

"For the sake of your work, I suppose."

"Is that so bad?"

Michael took off his glasses and cleaned them, taking his time over each lens. When he put them back on, his features were calm again. "Tell me, Tessa. Why haven't you ever done that session on Zen Buddhism? You've had plenty of opportunity in the years since we parted."

She pressed her lips together and looked away.

Michael sighed. "I'm glad to see you listened to me at least once." He lifted his menu again. "Do you want some suggestions on what to order?"

Her lips twitched. "I don't suppose there's anything with raw fish and seaweed?"

"Not that I know of." He didn't even look up.

Spoilsport. "Go ahead and order, Michael." She allowed herself a split-second glare. "I'm sure you know what's best."

Still no reaction.

Impossible man.

After he ordered, she said, "This Nonya food. What makes it so different?"

"Mrs. Ling cooks a dish that you could find at many Malay stalls, but with her own distinctive Nonya flavors. We can do a comparison one evening, if you'd like."

Which would mean another evening together. "We'll see. I'm pretty busy on location."

He inclined his head. "As you wish."

As you wish?

She stared at him for a stunned moment, then dropped her gaze to her lap. Westley's "I love you" from *The Princess Bride*. He had first spoken the words to her four years ago. She remembered the day perfectly, walking in the park past meticulously maintained Japanese gardens, sunlight around them, her hand held in his.

As you wish. Had he forgotten?

She plastered a bland smile across her face and lifted her gaze. He was watching her, waiting, though she couldn't tell for what. She panicked, flinging out her hand, and caught the top of her glass with her fingers.

"Oh, no." A giggle spurted up from between the fingers she pressed against her mouth. What an idiot. Talk about over-reacting.

Michael had stood immediately and was drying off his pants. He caught the chagrin in her eyes, grinned, then laughed out loud. "It was just an invitation, you know. A simple 'no, thanks' would have done the trick."

"Oh, Michael, I'm sorry."

"Forget it."

He dried off his chair and sat back down. The waiter brought more water and dry dishes. The food came, chicken and prawns and a vegetable combination cooked in coconut milk. Plenty of activity, but Tessa hardly noticed.

He *had* forgotten. It wasn't *The Princess Bride* he was quoting.

Her jaw stiffened. Why did that surprise her? He hadn't meant the words anyway, not even back then, not when real sacrifice was called for.

She took a few relaxing breaths and helped herself to some food. It all tasted surprisingly mild, with both a tangy sourness and hint of sweet. "This is quite good," she said.

He smiled. "But you would eat anything, I hear, including fried bugs."

"Jillian? When did you talk to her?"

"Last night on the phone."

Interesting. A friendly chat? Or something more? What was

their relationship anyway? She chewed her lip, glanced up, realized what she was doing, and changed the questions. "About Jillian. Why does she need money? She's rented a room to me, and she doesn't have the extras in her apartment that you do—including a maid. And even yesterday, during her shopping spree, she stuck to the sale racks. Why?"

"Tessa—"

"I know. You don't like to gossip. I'm just curious."

"Then ask her."

"Come on. I can't imagine it's anything bad—cocaine or gambling or anything like that."

Michael crossed his arms. "I suppose I'll have to tell you, if only to squelch ideas like that. The money's for her younger sister and brother. Her father left when she was a teenager. Her mother died when she was just finishing her own college degree. She would have gone on for an MBA, but got a job instead. Her sister wasn't even through high school, her brother barely begun."

So she was supporting her brother and sister. Tessa bit her lower lip. How admirable, but then Michael would hardly be interested in a woman without some finer qualities, would he?

"Don't worry about it," Michael said, misunderstanding her reaction completely. "You weren't to know."

Tessa winced. "Michael—"

But he was still speaking: "I've been wondering how I could help you get a feel for Singapore."

She backpedaled. "I'm not expecting you to arrange any-thing for me."

"Don't be foolish. Anywhere else you'd take advantage of contacts. Why not me?"

She opened her mouth but didn't know what to say.

"Well, Tessa?"

"You're busier, for one thing."

He waved the objection aside. "I'll manage. Tell me what you need."

Not having him around—that would help.

And yet what he said was true. She *would* make use of local contacts. Of course she would. So why not Michael?

It didn't have to mean more time together.

"All right, thank you. I need talkative tour guides mostly. People who know Singapore and won't mind my questions. Do you know anyone like that? Outspoken, opinionated, blunt, but friendly."

He cocked his head. "Someone like you, in other words."

"Michael..."

He grinned. "I'll think about it."

"And if you know a Singaporean who would be willing to tell me what it's like being a Christian here, that would be great, too."

"There's a woman at church. I think I can fix it." He nodded, and his smile grew. "This'll be interesting. I'm looking forward to it. Too bad you didn't get a job in Singapore sooner."

Good grief. She made a show of folding her napkin, lifting her bag, pushing her chair back. Anything to hide her surprise. Four years ago, he had sent her away because of photography, his decision firm and irrevocable, and now he was saying this? What else had he forgotten?

Outside, still thinking, he suggested hiring a taxi for the half day. "If you're ready to start your introduction to Singapore, I could show you around the island now."

"I don't think so, thank you." And just to resurrect some memories: "I have some work left over from my last assignment that I really must finish up."

"Ah." He nodded. "Then take this taxi. I have some work I could do at the bank myself."

She glanced back at him through the rear window. He was on his cell phone, presumably calling for another ride, apparently untouched by her verbal jab. She blew out a frustrated breath. *Give it up, Tessa.*

FIVE

Before returning to her apartment, Tessa purchased some snacks at one of the small grocery stores near Jillian's apartment—yogurt, a stash of Cadbury chocolate bars, bagels, peanut butter, and some fruit. The first half of a chocolate bar went down on the walk home, the second in the elevator. Tessa resisted opening another after putting her few groceries away and headed instead toward a cold shower and her most comfortable pair of jean shorts.

Those chocolate bars, her favorite quick fix for anxiety, had added most of the extra padding on her hips.

She spread out her Kazakhstan files on the coffee table and plugged in her lightbox, necessary for viewing the transparencies she had taken. Hours later, feeling pangs of hunger, she surfaced to discover it was 9:30 P.M. She toasted a bagel, spread some peanut butter on it, and returned to her work. When she turned off the light at 11:30, Jillian still hadn't returned.

Tessa woke early and stood for a moment at her door listening. Jillian was in the kitchen. The bathroom would be free.

Wearing only an oversized T-shirt and underwear, Tessa pushed open the bathroom door. A man stood at the sink, shaving.

"Oh! Sorry," Tessa said.

He wore boxer shorts and nothing else. Tessa backed away into the hallway.

"Morning, luv," the man said.

He was Australian, perhaps forty, quite muscular, and very good looking.

"Please, go ahead," Tessa said. "I'll wait."

His words drifted after her. "I'll be out in a jif."

Tessa shut her door and sank down onto her bed. Well, okay, she'd wear a robe after this.

Was this another reason why Michael had warned her against staying with Jillian? She frowned. Perhaps he didn't know that Jillian entertained overnight company.

Tessa heard talking in the kitchen, a low-pitched chuckle, Jillian's sharp response, more conversation, and eventually their departure.

She found a note on the kitchen table: *Sorry, too late last night to warn you. Maybe we can work out a signal.*

So there'd be more overnight visitors. Wonderful.

She fixed another bagel, then sat with it and her coffee next to the phone. Seven-thirty Monday morning in Singapore would be 5:30 Sunday afternoon in Chicago, a good time to call.

She hung up ten minutes later with a smile on her face.

A wonderfully uncomplicated man, her father was always glad to hear from her. Whether he remembered her existence between her calls, she couldn't say. All Andrew Brooks seemed to need was food for his belly, warmth for his body, and peace and quiet to think through his convoluted economic theories.

A victim herself of his benign neglect, Tessa could well understand why her mother Adrienne had left their home in suburban Chicago when Tessa was twelve. That she had left Tessa at the same time was another issue, one that Tessa had long ago decided not to dwell on.

She sat on the living room couch with her hands curled around her mug of coffee, savoring its warmth in the air-conditioned coolness of Jillian's apartment. The four years after her mother's departure had been hard years. Tessa had taken care of both her father and herself, carting groceries from a nearby store, using paper plates as often as not, and badgering her father over the few details of their simple lives that she couldn't handle herself. She'd had few friends and spent hours alone.

Then one summer afternoon, when she was fourteen, she found her father's old Leica camera, and since that day, photography had been her passion, her joy, her most loyal companion. When Tessa was sixteen, her father had married Jenny Duvall, one of his graduate students at the University of Chicago and the person who introduced them both to Jesus Christ. Tessa turned over her father's care to Jenny and spent the next two years chasing photographs for the local newspaper, developing them in her basement darkroom, selling enough to buy new lenses and equipment.

Had it not been for Jenny, Tessa might have dropped out of school completely. But Jenny loved Tessa's photography. She insisted on hanging her best prints along the hall in the foyer, where everyone entering would see them. And whenever Tessa had new work to show, Jenny set aside the dishes or the cooking or even her research on the computer to sit at the kitchen table and study each one. Tessa remembered it so clearly, Jenny's hand smoothing over the plastic sleeves, as if blessing the people themselves, and not just Tessa.

Through it all, Jenny kept saying the same thing to Tessa over and over again: "God has given you this talent for a reason. Don't bury it in the ground. Use it, develop it. Become the best photographer you can be—all for the glory of God."

Tessa had taken the words to heart and managed somehow to finish high school with her classmates and even made plans for college.

Her mother, in the meantime, had been in law school. Soon

after passing the New York bar exam, Adrienne Brooks had married Charles Webster, a high-powered electronics executive who lived in Japan. Tessa agreed to visit when she was eighteen—and then only because Jenny gave her no peace about refusing. That's when she had first met Michael.

Tessa leaned her head back against the sofa.

She was old enough now to understand and even forgive her father's obsessions, her mother's ultimate flight, the inevitable consequences for herself. Old enough to forgive, if not always to ignore the wounds.

Let it go, she told herself, and reached for the phone again. Corin would be back in New York by now. He was always good for a lift in spirits.

"Hey, Wander Woman, thanks for calling," he said. "I'm glad you found me."

"How was Mount Erebus?"

"What do you think? Cold." She could hear his smile. "But I made it back, all in one piece, even if I am still thawing."

"And the photos?"

"Worth every minute. I turned them in to the *Adventure* editor on Tuesday. Alpenglow, ice towers around the crater, icebergs in the Ross Sea—all good stuff. And the Nikon F4 worked great, as long as I wired the battery packs under my parka."

"I have the opposite problem here. Too much humidity and lots of heat."

"Yeah—imagine that. It's a big world, isn't it? Otherwise, things okay?"

"I'm renting a room from someone my cousin works with. It's much cheaper than the Hyatt Regency."

"Is she Singaporean?"

"No. She's from Ohio. Cleveland, I think. A loan officer at my cousin's bank."

"Super. Say hello to Michael, by the way. Always good to have a banker in the family. Say, I'm doing that shoot on volcanos next, in Indonesia. Maybe I'll drop by for a visit."

"When?"

"Would your Cleveland friend mind me bunking down on the couch?"

Tessa balked. Considering last night's company…

"What was I thinking?" Corin said. "That would offend your sensibilities, wouldn't it? I'm almost glad, you know. It gives me hope that somewhere behind those Victorian traditions you're just a little bit tempted. How about your cousin then? Could he put me up?"

"I could ask him. When would you come?"

"This weekend. I've got these two assignments back to back, hardly a week between them, but I'd love to see you. It's been a while. Now I have to go—a party my photo rep wants me to show up at. I'm half an hour late already. Call me back, okay? You know I love you."

Tessa hung up the phone and pulled a throw pillow to her chest. Michael and Corin, together—what a thought.

She had met Corin Bolt at a workshop. He was giving the class on adventure photography; she on travel. A smile, an invitation, a late-night dinner, and he'd been ready to take her to bed. Even now, after almost three years of refusals, he still couldn't fathom how she lived without sex.

"Anxiety, nothing," he'd said, the first time he'd seen her on location. "Those chocolate bars are masking another problem entirely. Why don't you let me solve it the old-fashioned way?"

Even less did he understand her commitment to Jesus Christ.

Yet, for all their differences, his was the face she sought at any gathering of photographers, his was the smile, his the approval.

And what a contrast to Michael.

Corin never complained about her travel schedule, his own being just as bad. He never faulted her passion for photography, her drive to succeed. And after all these years he kept trying. He had even mentioned marriage the last time they'd seen each other in October.

She smiled, remembering: "Aren't you afraid we're not compatible?" she'd said. "Without having a chance to check it out, I mean?"

"Listen, babe, you can trust me. I've yet to meet the woman—"

"Stop." She'd held up her hand. "I don't want to hear it."

The laughter had vanished from his eyes. He'd taken her hands in his and kissed first one and then the other. "And yet I'd be faithful, Tessa. For you, I would."

She went to the kitchen and poured herself a glass of guava juice, sipping it as she leaned back against the counter.

She believed Corin, at least believed he would try. Faithfulness in marriage wasn't necessarily linked to being a Christian—of course not. But faithfulness to Jesus Christ was, and how could she give herself wholeheartedly to any man who didn't share a relationship with him?

Now Michael—

But no, it did no good to dwell on Michael either. He shared her commitment to Christ, but not her commitment to photography. He wanted his own Jenny, someone to be home for him, who would put his schedule in red ink on the calendar, her own in pencil around his, and Tessa refused to comply.

Michael and Corin: Only enough merit between the two of

them to make one good sort of man—now where had she read that?—but neither alone would do.

Her heart still gave a queer little leap when the phone rang shortly after nine, and when she heard Michael say her name that same treacherous heart seemed to melt in a ridiculous puddle.

Hearts leaping and melting into puddles?

She rolled her eyes.

"Yes," she said, keeping her voice bland. "It's me."

"Good. For that tour, how about a Buddhist temple? I called someone I know, a professor from the university, who said he could spare a few hours around noon. He's exactly as you described—outspoken, knowledgeable, more than willing to share his opinions and beliefs. His name is Simon Hwang and he suggested meeting at the Temple of Ten Thousand Lights on Race Course Road."

"How will we recognize each other?"

"I'll come, too."

"You don't have to, Michael."

"Simon's expecting me."

"Okay, then. I'll see you there."

Her taxi headed north on Serangoon Street, through the heart of Little India, passing cross streets with names like Veeraswamy and Hindoo and Baboo. Tessa wondered about finding a Buddhist temple here, then smiled at her doubts. Buddhism had begun in India, after all, even if it had been swallowed up there pretty quickly by Hinduism.

Michael stood with his friend near the entrance of the temple. Simon Hwang looked young to be a professor, mid-thirties, perhaps.

And very friendly.

He stepped forward without waiting for an introduction from Michael. "Welcome to Singapore, Miss Brooks. I'm Simon Hwang."

"Tessa, please."

Simon held her gaze a moment, a definite gleam in his eyes. "Tessa it is, then. I've seen your work, you know. I stopped by the university library this morning specifically for that reason."

"How nice of you."

"Not at all. I had to check you out for myself. I've made it my policy not to take Michael's word for anything."

"Michael?" Tessa glanced sideways. Michael appeared relaxed, looking down at the sidewalk, arms crossed, a hint of a smile playing across his features. "What has he been saying?"

Simon laughed. "He was quick to deny a blood-relationship, for one. Step-cousins, didn't you say, Michael?"

Michael cleared his throat. "Time to go in if we want to see anything."

Simon laughed again.

Inside the Temple of Ten Thousand Lights, a huge fifty-foot statue of a decidedly Oriental Buddha dominated the scene. He sat cross-legged, in the classic pose for meditation, gazing off into the distance. His yellow skin gleamed under the light from high windows, and a nimbus of electric bulbs outlined his figure. The thousand lights, Tessa realized. She asked Simon about taking photographs, then clicked off a few shots.

Simon talked as she worked. "The entire complex—the statue, the walls, even the tigers at the gate—were built by a single Thai monk named Vutthisasara. Before he died you could find him here every day, teaching Buddhist doctrine and philosophy. His paintings around the pedestal show scenes from the Buddha's life. Come and see."

The paintings were no more than she expected, stylized and somewhat simplistic, an act of devotion, not art. She looked instead toward the side rooms where she heard the chanting of Buddhist monks, saw people kneeling at altars, children and women busying themselves in worship. The difficulties of composition intrigued her, especially the many vertical lines—red and gold banners from the ceiling, tall red candles, hanging tapestries on the wall. In Christianity, those vertical lines would point toward heaven. What did they point to here?

Simon had followed her away from the central statue of Buddha. "Are you a Protestant Christian, Tessa Brooks, like Michael?"

She smiled and nodded.

"Then this kind of worship must seem foreign to you. You Protestants always want a group, don't you?"

"For church services, yes." She sensed Michael beside her, knew he was close enough now to hear.

"In Asia," Simon said, "people choose their own paths, without any Western urgency for group consensus. You evangelicals can't survive on your own, which must be why you're constantly trying to add to your numbers."

Tessa blinked. So much for charm.

"The group gives your faith validity," he said.

"Perhaps."

"Look." Simon watched with Tessa as a woman and a small boy knelt before an altar. The priest took an offering from each, did something at the altar that she couldn't see, and began chanting a prayer. "Buddhist worship stresses inward concentration and meditation," he said. "What counts occurs within, an inner spirituality."

"Without any reference to God?"

"Spoken like a true theist. What do you know of Buddhism?

Have you heard of the Four Noble Truths?"

"Behold the professor," Michael said.

Tessa nudged him into silence. "I can name them: Life is filled with suffering. We suffer because of wrongly directed desires. We can eliminate the suffering by eliminating the wrong desires. We can do that by following the Eightfold Path." Anticipating Simon's question, she shook her head. "No, I can't name all those."

"You did better than many of my students, sometimes even after lectures. You must have done some study."

She glanced at Michael. "Not as much as I might have liked."

"Wrong desires," he whispered, "which someone helped you eliminate."

Simon had walked closer to a huge brass urn in which sticks of incense burned. "Come here, Tessa. Do you see the smoke curling up, rising, and then gone? This, to me, symbolizes the central truth of Buddhism. You know what I'm speaking of, don't you, Michael?"

"The pervasive impermanence of all life."

"No, no, Michael. You haven't been listening. The form of life changes, but life itself continues, moving from one expression to another, ceaselessly flowing in a smooth unending transition. I've told you this many times: Try to hold on to one form, and you will always suffer. Let go and you'll achieve peace."

Tessa looked from one man to the other. She was surprised to see Michael suffer Simon's dictums so patiently.

"How do you two know each other, anyway?" she said.

"Simon's father is a client," Michael answered. "When I heard that Simon taught comparative religion at the university, I asked him to come speak to my Bible study group on Buddhism."

"That's only half the story," Simon said. "I made the mistake of playing golf with him. It turns out I'm one of the few people Michael can consistently beat."

Michael grinned. "It's true."

They had walked back to the open central area in front of the statue of Buddha.

"As for your study," Simon said, "I managed to get a few of them wavering, didn't I?"

"You got them interested, certainly."

"Most of your study members have no idea what their native religions teach. A few words of explanation to the Buddhist converts, a few pointed questions about what you were saying, and they saw the value of Buddhist teaching." He wagged his finger at Michael, and though his lips still smiled, his eyes had grown serious. "You're taking them backward in their path toward enlightenment."

"I'm affirming what every person knows in his heart—that he's real and significant and special."

"I know, I know, a treasure loved by God himself. You've told me all this before. But this notion of a personal God hinders growth. You should get beyond that, Michael."

"And abandon my own personality—my very self—in the process?"

"Wrong desires, Michael. Wrong desires."

"But it *might* be true," Tessa said. "God might be real. He might have come to earth and lived among us."

Simon gave a benign smile. "Pursue what you now understand, Tessa. Perhaps you'll reach a greater understanding in the future."

"You mean the next time around."

"Tessa—" Michael said.

"No! He's saying we can believe whatever we want, but if

we're good enough we'll end up Buddhists eventually."

Michael took her hand and squeezed it.

Simon was looking very superior now, with that painted Chinese smile that meant he was embarrassed for her sake. "Only by abandoning the self and all its desires can we achieve true peace."

"Your peace sounds like a real blast," Tessa said. "Of anesthesia. What about joy and happiness, loving and being loved, knowing and being known? Are those such bad desires?"

Simon wagged his finger again. "You sound like Michael, both of you so convinced that your God knows you and loves you. In a small way, I envy you this idea of a personal relationship, but wisdom soon prevails. I know too many unhappy Christians. Better to fight desire completely than to be so consistently disappointed."

Tessa's chin went up. "And I thought comparative religions tried to see the value in all beliefs."

Simon drew back, and then laughed, this time a little ruefully. "Hoist on my own dogma. Well done, Miss Tessa Brooks."

She took a breath, struggling to relax, and managed a stiff smile.

"But don't be upset with me," Simon said. "It's all Michael's fault. Just look at him. He's too sure of himself."

"Now *that* I can understand." Tessa crossed her arms, and together she and Simon studied Michael. "He often has the same effect on me."

"Hey," Michael said, "are we finished here or what?"

Simon laughed. "Indeed we are. I appreciate the invitation to lunch, Michael, but I must get back to campus for a lecture this afternoon. Nice meeting you, Tessa."

He nodded in response to her thanks, shook hands with Michael, and left.

Tessa blew out a whistling breath. "He sure pushed a few of my buttons. Is he actually Buddhist?"

"If by 'actually' you mean exclusively Buddhist, no. Simon's not exclusively anything, which is why evangelical Christianity offends him so much. He doesn't like the notion that there's only one way to God."

"And yet he defends Buddhism well enough."

"He knows the theory, that's for sure, and, as you heard, is always ready to use it against Christianity. Whether he owns it for himself, I don't know." He pointed to the temple entrance. "Ready to go?"

Outside Tessa glanced back up the stairs to the temple. "Do you ever think they might be right?"

"Buddhists? All truth is God's truth, wherever we find it. Their teaching includes much that we would agree with—dying to self, finding happiness in serving others, showing compassion. As for eliminating desires, that does offer a tempting solution to our frustrations."

"But…?"

"The peace they seek is tranquillity. The peace we need is reconciliation, a cessation of hostilities between God and us."

Tessa nodded. "His Buddhism sounds too much like Valium on the battlefield."

"Exactly, with disastrous consequences." Michael frowned. "Maybe it's my Western mentality, or maybe I do have an inflated sense of my own importance…"

He paused.

"Yes?"

"I keep picturing a scene in hell, Satan and his cohorts planning strategy. They've mapped out Western self-obsession—man the measure of all things, God in the distance if he exists at all. And Satan says, 'That's not bad enough. These Western humanists may not worship God, but they still value themselves and inadvertently give him glory since they're his creation. Let's go even further in the East. Let's propose the idea that God is completely unknowable and that the extinction of self should be a primary goal. That will rob God on both counts.' And so you have Buddhism," Michael said, "a gradual retreat into complete non-existence." He shook his head. "Jehovah God wants to redeem selfhood, not extinguish it. And he wants us to know him even as we are known."

Tessa grinned. "Satan, huh? I hope you didn't share that scenario with Simon."

"Hardly, though he knows well enough where I stand. Now, before we both melt under this heat and humidity, do you have time for lunch? Since we're in Little India anyway, how about the Banana Leaf Apollo? It's just down the road, and from what I hear, has the perfect blend of horrible decor and great cuisine—Singaporeans, you know, think that a lavish interior means bad food."

"Lead on."

SIX

A confusion of colors assaulted Tessa when she entered the Banana Leaf Apollo. Formica tables filled the room, with garishly embellished tiles reaching waist-high around the walls. Nothing looked new. The blues were fading; the tiles were chipped; some of the chairs sported Band-Aids of duct tape.

"By your maxim," Tessa whispered to Michael, "the food must be fabulous."

They decided to eat vegetarian and ended up with rice for Tessa, and crisply fried rice pancakes called *dosai* for Michael, with a variety of spicy sauces called *sambar* to share, and eggplant, lentil, potato, green beans, and cabbage. For a plate, the waiter spread a banana leaf in front of each of them. Michael would have asked for cutlery, but Tessa discouraged him. "How can it taste authentic if we don't use our fingers?"

They went to wash their hands. After a silent prayer, she opened her eyes and found Michael watching her. She managed a smile, one she hoped looked calm, and began working her food together, pulling a little of the *sambar* over onto the rice.

There was so much between them, so much they should probably discuss, and yet at every opportunity she found herself unable to broach the hard subjects. Thank goodness for Singapore's food. Such a welcome diversion.

She shoved a quick mixture of *sambar* and rice in her mouth, choked at the fiery spices, and grabbed desperately for her glass of water.

"That won't help," Michael said. "Eat some yogurt, if you need something."

"It's really hot! Hotter than any Indian food I remember."

"Hotter weather in the South. Hotter food as well. Should I order something milder?"

"No, it's fine. Thank you for bringing me here." She took another bite, coughed, and managed to resist the water this time. "Simon seems to have a very low opinion of Christianity."

"Mostly he thinks it's easy. And he's right. Christianity is the easiest of all religions since we're saved by God's action, not our own. Simon just refuses to acknowledge how hard grace is to swallow."

"Especially for Asians. The ultimate loss of face."

"Especially for anyone, you mean. Who wants to be that dependent on someone else's generosity? And yet it's not just grace we have to accept, but his right to command as well. Simon would rather do away with a personal God entirely than admit he owes God allegiance. And he's not alone."

"He loses a lot," she said.

"He loses everything."

She looked around the crowded restaurant. People were eating, talking, laughing together. They looked happy. "Everything?"

"What will it profit a man..."

She blew out a long breath and scooted her banana leaf away. The food wasn't going down well, anyway.

"Sorry," he said. "The food or the topic?"

"A little of both, I suppose, but it's okay. I've been eating too much anyway." Following Michael's example, she dipped her hand in the small bowl of water provided for that purpose and wiped it dry. "It's amazing how much food is figuring in my experience of Singapore."

"Sometimes I think the cuisine is all Singapore has going for it."

"Surely not," she said. "It's also clean and safe and efficient."

"Clean, yes, to the point of being sterile. Have you noticed how few flowers Singapore has? Orchids, that's what Singapore is known for, and very fitting, I think. They're so cold and exotic."

She smiled. "You're definitely not a Buddhist, Michael."

"What do you mean?"

"You'd rather have weeds with the wildflowers than no flowers at all."

"Maybe." He nodded. "Yes. You're right. That's it exactly. But you'll see what I mean. It takes a while, but there's something missing here."

After Michael returned to his office, Tessa put on her cap, made her way over to Serangoon Street in the heart of Indian Singapore, and spent the afternoon taking photographs. Knowing she could sell a photo essay on the colorful street, she decided to return sometime during the week and spend an entire day there, from early, early morning through the evening. She picked up an Indonesian noodle dish on her way home and began working on her photo choices for Kazakhstan again.

Around 8:00, Jillian slipped in with Hugo, her Australian friend. "I'll shower first," she told him, "then you can take a turn. Have a drink while you're waiting."

He came over to Tessa instead. "What you got there, luv?"

"Some shots I took on my last assignment. I'm choosing which ones to send on to the client."

"That's right. You're a photographer. Show me the way it works." He held up a page of transparencies. "Which of these would you say were worth the effort?"

Tessa spent the next thirty minutes pointing out the details of composition and lighting and angles and balance that made the difference between a good shot and a great one. By the time Jillian emerged in a flared chartreuse dress, Hugo was ready to take a stab at picking out the best on an unmarked sheet.

"This one," he said.

Tessa took the sheet from him, shook her head, and tapped her own choice.

"Go on! You can't even see the bloke's face, just his shoulder, and the other one's looking off who knows where."

Tessa laughed. "But you see their strength, the way this one's straining to open the valves, the dirt on his hands and arms, and the rip in this other guy's jacket. The one looking away emphasizes how lonely the work is, and the glare reflecting off both the snow and the sweat on this guy's face—Hugo, this is a great shot, exactly what my client wanted."

"Yeah? Let me try another one."

"Hey." Jillian leaned over close to Hugo, exuding a musky fragrance. "Remember me?"

"Sorry, luv. Sure. Quick stop in the loo, and I'll be with you." He stumbled up but kept the last contact sheet in hand. He studied the frames, then shook his head. "Beats me." He handed it back to Tessa. "Out in a minute, luv."

Jillian went to the mirror by the door and adjusted her wide shoulder straps a little lower on her arms. "He's cute, isn't he? I do love these burly types with plenty of muscle on their shoulders. He's on shore leave from a freighter. It adds a delicious sense of danger to the whole transaction, don't you think—knowing they have that power at bay?"

"I suppose." Tessa reached for another transparency sheet.

"Something wrong?"

"How long have you known him?"

"I met him Saturday night. He's shipping out again in the morning."

"Oh."

Jillian turned to stare at Tessa, who was still busy with her work. "You have a problem with that?"

Tessa looked up. "I wouldn't want it for myself, no, but it's your choice."

"Good, cuz—"

Hugo breezed in, unaware of the tension between Tessa and Jillian. "I'm ready." He came back to the table and picked up the disputed contact sheet again. "You know, it grows on you, this one with the shoulders. I think I understand what you were getting at."

"Come on," Jillian said, "or we won't have any time to dance."

Hugo stuck out his hand to Tessa. "Nice to meet you, Tessa Brooks, and thanks for the lesson. Makes me want to drag out my own camera, you know?"

In the quiet after they left, Tessa gave a wry smile. Of course she had a problem with what Jillian was doing. Hugo was nice, and curious, too, which showed his intelligence, but to get into bed after knowing him only one weekend?

Tessa rubbed her forehead. Was she a coward not to confront Jillian?

And yet she had been honest with Jillian as well. From the beginning, with Adam and Eve, God had allowed people to choose their own way, somehow working out his will at the same time. If he allowed the weeds, why shouldn't Tessa?

She woke Tuesday morning with the frustrating sense of holding onto a dream. Her father had been in it and Charles as well.

But at the moment of waking, Blake dominated her thoughts most of all.

Why Blake?

She pushed herself up on an elbow.

They'd been dancing together, incredibly, his arms so tight around her chest that she couldn't get away. In real life they were almost the same height, but here he towered over her. And in that crazy, helpless way of dreams, she couldn't get her eyes open to look at Blake. She could see everyone else in the room, even Michael behind her, but not Blake. She'd been trying to, tugging up on her heavy eyelids, the sense of danger and fear building, trying to get her arms free...when she woke.

She plopped her head back onto the pillow and held her arms outstretched above her. *Blake Hoffman—man of my dreams.*

She groaned. *Man of my nightmares.*

Big help you were, Michael Lawton.

In the hall outside her room, Tessa met Jillian, fully dressed, coming out of the bathroom.

"Hugo's gone. He had to be on board by 6 A.M. How'd you like to go get some breakfast since I'm up already?"

"I'd love to. Just give me a minute."

Tessa put on a T-shirt and short overalls and joined Jillian in a taxi to Newton Circus, a massive outdoor food center only minutes by taxi from Jillian's apartment.

In times past, Tessa knew, poor immigrants had made their living pushing carts of food around Singapore, selling their spicy delicacies to passing pedestrians. For health reasons, the city had now installed the hawkers in pristine, well-lit food centers. Newton Circus was one of the biggest.

Amazed at the array of stalls—almost a hundred—Tessa left Jillian at her favorite fruit stand and walked around the large arena, breathing in the pungent odors of garlic and ginger, cumin and turmeric, pepper and soy sauce. She had expected the variety. She had not anticipated the confusion of sounds— stall owners calling to each other and to the customers, steam hissing and rising in sudden huge spurts, the sharp tones of Mandarin mingling with the musical tones of Bahasa Malay. Entranced, she twisted her cap around and shot three rolls of film.

At Jillian's fruit stand, the lavish array caught Tessa's eye. The man behind the counter stepped closer. "Yes, hallo, you like fluit juice. Only one dollah, hallo."

Tessa smiled and nodded, then realized he was waiting for her to choose which fruit she wanted in her drink. Pineapple, papaya, and mango, she decided. Tessa's first thought on tasting the luscious mixture was to wonder if Michael had ever tasted something like it.

She squelched the thought. She still hadn't asked Michael about Corin staying over for a few nights, and she wasn't ready to explore why.

She took the drink back to the table where Jillian sat eating a plate of papaya and rolls.

"I've been watching you photograph," Jillian said. "It's an athletic profession if nothing else. It took a lot of guts to climb up on that rickety chair."

"Strong angles, every photographer wants them. They require looking at the subject from all directions, and usually the best is the one most people don't see. Good pictures give a fresh perspective to life."

"And so you squat and get flat on your face and climb up on rickety chairs?"

"I'd have stood on the table itself if I weren't so scared of getting a fine."

"Smart girl," Jillian said. "But tell me one thing: With all those gymnastics, how do you keep people from posing?"

"Outdoor shopping like this is perfect. The hawkers have no choice but to keep working, and the shoppers are too intent on breakfast to spend much time looking at me." Tessa waved a hand to the people around them. "Early morning has the added advantage of everyone being fresh and dressed for work."

"You enjoy it."

"I love it. Most of the time, I can't imagine doing anything else."

"Is there *any* down side to the job?"

"Tired muscles, muddled connections, rushed timetables, lost luggage, lousy weather, missed shots, ruined film…" Tessa laughed. "Tell me when to stop. The technical side takes practice. The composition takes an artistic eye, a certain way of looking. But when I come into a crowd like this, my biggest problem is inertia. That first contact of the day is the hardest, walking up cold to someone I don't know and convincing them to let me take their picture." She lifted her fruit drink in salute. "I'd much rather just sit here."

"Why not take pictures with a zoom lens, then? They'd never know you were there."

Across from Tessa a spry Chinese man, clad in a sleeveless T-shirt, shorts, and thongs, was spooning soup into bowls, shouting jokes and jibes at coworkers and customers, laughing often. His name, Tessa knew, was Goh Fong Lee, and he had lived in Singapore his entire life, born to a Chinese father and a Straits-born wife. Could she have taken as good a picture without first establishing rapport with him? Would she have managed to catch his gap-toothed smile, the happy flick of his wrist as the ladle emptied?

"Each person is special," Tessa said in response to Jillian's question. "To capture that uniqueness I have to know them, at least a little. Not that it always works. For some people, one glimpse of my camera and they tell me to get lost." She glanced around. "Fortunately, not today."

"But you like roaming around like this, no home, no family?"

Tessa hesitated. "Most of the time."

"I would, too," Jillian said. "Especially the no responsibilities part."

"I can understand that. Michael told me about supporting your sisters."

"One sister, one brother. Want to see?" Jillian displayed a wallet photo of a dark-eyed girl laughing into the camera. "This is Lisa. She's graduating from Ohio State this year, on her way to becoming an architect. I'm so proud of her I could burst."

"And your brother?"

"He's playing minor league ball. I doubt Jace'll ever make the majors, but who cares? He's happy, you know, and that's okay."

"What about you? How long will you stay in Singapore?"

"As long as the bank's willing to have me." A cloud came over her face. "Which since Blake arrived, might not be much longer. I just wish I had his ability to get in good with the executive bunch. He's constantly playing golf with one of the vice presidents and being invited to go boating with a client, and that silky smooth accent doesn't hurt any, either. I can't even say it's gender bias; he really is good at what he does." She scowled across the table at Tessa, then shrugged. "Anyway, yeah, I hope to stick around long enough to pay off Lisa's college bills—one more good bonus should do it. And on that note, I better get going."

Tessa stayed longer, trading smiles with a friendly toddler, talking with his mother, getting advice on what else to eat for breakfast from two Singapore University students. These last, two women, were on their way to campus and agreed to give Tessa a tour. When they left for class, she found a seat in one of the pavilions and stayed there until noon, enjoying conversation as it came.

There was a time when being on any campus would have caused her discomfort. She came from a family of intellectuals after all—her father a professor, her mother with a law degree, her stepmother with a doctorate. Even Charles came from an educational elite, amassing honorary degrees to go with his earned ones. Tessa had made it through only two semesters of college. At the beginning of her first summer break, she had begged money from her father, grabbed her camera, and headed out to Thailand to visit a friend working in a refugee camp. Someone from Terry's agency had seen her photographs and published a selection in a fund-raising appeal. That led to two years at a newspaper job. After an additional year of training, working as an assistant to a well-heeled and demanding photo-essayist, she felt ready to branch out on her own. It had taken two years longer to get her first major assignment.

She grimaced. That was in Japan, shortly after Michael had proposed.

She tipped her head up and let her eyes wander the skyline. Here were buildings and people, the sounds and smells of this particular city's life—Singapore. She let her imagination wander further, into the Malaysian forests beyond the horizon and then Thailand and the mountain tribes of Myanmar, and in the other direction toward Indonesia and Australia or the South Pacific islands, knowing that over all those hills, across each expanse of water and around every corner, something special and interesting and real waited for her.

She had felt it so sharply back then—life changing, dancing, a celebration of God's creative energy and exuberance. How could she have resisted the call to that celebration four years ago? It was her chance to prove herself, to offer something of value to life, to the world, even to God.

And now? She sighed. The early rush had been wonderful, and it was Michael's misfortune to get swept aside by it, but lately, with success came questions. It all seemed too much an automated exercise—colors, composition, f-stops, light source—with the camera always between her and the life she longed to celebrate, letting her see and record but never take part. Where had that early joy gone?

Upset at her ingratitude—who had given her the talent, anyway, or the opportunity to develop it?—she taxied back to Jillian's apartment, retrieved her Kazakhstan photographs, and took them to the photo shop recommended by Asia Premier Publications. She spent the rest of the afternoon wandering through Singapore's art galleries, a habit she had picked up long ago as a source of inspiration.

Around four she sat down wearily on a park bench. Perhaps she was just feeling jet lag. Or perhaps it was time for that extended break Corin kept encouraging her to take. She could spend some time in Chicago with her father and Jenny, taking care of the business end of her career. And then maybe a long, lazy vacation. That might help her remember why she loved photography so much.

Or perhaps she just needed something new to think about.

Blake came to mind. That's what she would do. She'd try to solve this puzzle, get her subconscious off her back, and stop the dreams. She glanced at her watch. If she stopped by Chadsworth now, she might catch another unguarded response from him and maybe even get a picture of him, something to study. Perhaps she *had* met him before.

Detective Tessa Brooks, no case too obscure. But it would get her mind off both photography and Michael, for at least a little while.

Michael heard her speak his name, no doubt to the receptionist sitting in front of the elevators, before he saw her. Grateful for the warning, he saved his file and stood to meet her. "Tessa."

She wore loose pale green slacks and a sleeveless buttoned vest, all in some soft, flowing material that hugged her curves and gave her a sophisticated elegance.

"Hello, Michael. Jillian. Nigel's already gone?"

But through all of her greetings, Michael noticed, she kept her eyes on Blake. She even took a step toward his desk.

"Blake. How are you?"

Jillian intercepted her before Blake could answer. "You got more sun today. What happened to your White Sox cap?"

Tessa rubbed her nose. "I wore it most of the day."

"White Sox?" Michael said.

She pulled the cap out of her backpack. "My father's favorite team, don't ask me why. I wear it for the black color." She smiled at his confusion. "I stand out enough taking pictures, don't you think? Add to that blond hair in a crowd of Asians, and you see why I need some camouflage."

Michael grinned. "Then the red nose doesn't help. You might want to try a parasol—a large one."

"Or one of those huge floppy sun hats Katherine Hepburn wore in *The African Queen,*" Jillian added.

As they were speaking, Blake rose and slipped past Tessa out of the office.

"Where'd he go?"

"To talk to the secretary?" Michael said. "File room? Maybe the bathroom?"

Tessa continued to frown. "You know…" she started, then shook her head. "Oh well." Her gaze shifted to the scene outside the eighteenth floor window. "Wow, look at that sun."

Michael's office faced north from Robinson Road and a little east, and so received little direct sunlight in the afternoon. But late in the day, the skyscrapers along Collyer Quay caught the light of the descending sun and reflected it back through the bank of windows facing his desk. Until Tessa had come in, Michael hadn't taken much notice of the dazzling brilliance.

"And those storm clouds gathering off toward the north," Tessa said. "They're great. I've got to get a picture." She spun around to face Michael. "Any chance I can go up on the roof, or perhaps a balcony?"

He glanced at his watch. Five thirty.

"I could try through your windows," she said, "but it would be so much better…"

"There's a terrace two floors up."

"Let's take the stairs. They'll be faster."

He pulled the stairwell door open. "Why the rush?"

"It's the clouds." She hurried past him. "They're moving in fast. Oh, this is nice."

The terrace, about thirty feet deep, topped one end of the building. Bushes and potted trees provided shade, and a pleasant breeze blew. Tessa set up her tripod. "Are the tables for you—I mean, the people who work at Chadsworth?"

"For clients and special occasions. We sometimes have meals catered up here, and of course cocktails."

"It's perfect for me. Thank you, Michael."

He watched as she zipped open her carry-all, extracted a filter, adjusted her settings, and then took what must have been an entire roll of film, shifting her tripod around the terrace as she continued. It didn't take her long.

"I'll just try one other lens," she said, "if you don't mind."

But she wasn't really asking.

He clenched his jaw. That camera. How well he remembered. At any moment she might reach for it—absently, instinctively, a source of comfort and security. And once she started with the pictures, that's when her feelings really showed. She would cradle the body in the palm of her hand, caress the lenses, stroke the dials.... He stifled a groan.

Four years ago at twenty-eight, he had fantasized often about throwing the thing on the ground and jumping on it like a spoiled child until it broke.

At thirty-two, apparently, not much had changed.

She turned, her eyes shining. "I'm done. The shot's probably trite and overdone, but I had to try. Now, come closer, Michael. Show me your city. What is that big flat building over there with the brown roof?"

"I don't have time, Tessa." He cleared his throat and tried again. "I'm meeting a client. Sorry. I'm late already."

"Michael! You should have told me. Go ahead, please."

"Were you here to meet Jillian?"

"Or you. For dinner." They had reached the office, empty now. "It doesn't matter."

He glanced up and down the hallway.

"Something else wrong?" she said.

"Just looking for Blake. We're meeting this client together. He must have gotten tired of waiting."

Tessa clutched her photo bag against her side. "Then you better hurry. I'll call you later."

"I should at least ride down with you."

"Oh. Security. Sure."

He pushed the button for the lobby. He was beginning to feel foolish. "I'm sorry about dinner. What will you do now?"

She smiled. "You know, I think I might go see a movie. It's been forever."

"Ah."

They stepped out under the overhang in front of the building. It had already begun to rain. "Those clouds did move in fast," she said. "But look, here's your taxi. Go ahead. I'll be all right."

Michael climbed in, gave the location for the business dinner he had scheduled, then sat back against the seat cushion. Of course she'd be all right. That was the whole problem. When had Tessa Brooks ever needed anyone or anything—except her camera and a reason to use it? The question was, would that ever change?

He tipped his head forward. *I don't know, Father, but you do. Help me out, please, if you will. You can touch her heart in a way I only dream of doing.*

But judging from his reaction to her work, he, too, had changed little in four years. An obsession, he had called it once before to her face, an accusation he still regretted. He could only hope she hadn't noticed his impatience, or if she had that she credited it to being late for his appointment.

So I need your mercy as well, Father. Touch my heart, too.

Instead of a movie, Tessa headed home and flopped onto the couch in the living room. What an awkward encounter. If she had wanted to put him out of her mind, Chadsworth hadn't been a very sensible place to go.

Blake, anyway, had behaved according to form, which still confused her. With each passing day, in fact, with each bizarre encounter, the question became more pressing: Why was he avoiding her? She couldn't help but feel it was something she needed to find out.

She knew where to begin looking for the answer. She stashed her photo gear in her bedroom and pulled out her portfolios instead. A review of past work might spur her memory.

Nothing.

Still determined, she opened her laptop and called up a list of her assignments, starting all the way back in high school when she photographed for the local paper and proceeding through to Kazakhstan. Had she really done so much? She scrolled through entry after entry, name after name, reading the entire log.

Still nothing. Except a saddened heart.

She rubbed a hand across her eyes. So many people, so many conversations, encounters, exchanges…all gone. She had bragged to Jillian about establishing some kind of rapport with the people she photographed, yet how many hundreds of people had passed silently out of her memory? A spark of interest, a smile, a click or two of the shutter to get the image she wanted, and then good-bye.

And she actually imagined, out of all these people drifting in and out of her life, she would remember one face like Blake Hoffman's and be able to mark him?

SEVEN

"Miss Brooks? I am Miss Chen. Please come with me."

From the steps of the Singaporean school, the young Miss Chen took Tessa first to Mr. Lim, the principal, and then to Mrs. Yeh, the teacher whose preschool class Tessa would be photographing.

She welcomed the day's assignment. Michael's behavior at his office the previous evening had upset her more than seemed sensible, and failing to discover anything about Blake hadn't helped. Today would take care of those feelings. Children always raised her spirits.

Mrs. Yeh, stern-faced and fortyish, clapped her hands for attention, and the children gathered around to hear who Tessa was and what she did. Then, as arranged, Mrs. Yeh let Tessa talk to the children herself.

"I'm so happy to be here," Tessa said, and it was true. The bright faces of the Singaporean children—healthy, well-fed, rested, and alert—would make the visit a special treat.

She opened her photography bag and laid out the supplies from her backpack—three camera bodies, five different lenses, her two flash attachments, tripod, film, and a log book. A few minutes of showing how she fit the pieces together, a shine or two from her flash attachment, and the children were ready to see some slides. She carried pictures of children for just such occasions—funny ones, poignant, silly, and a few sad, chosen to show how children the world over shared the same emotions. With the slide show as an introduction, now that they knew what she was doing, the children happily relaxed in front of her camera and returned to their work.

Much later, after five, Tessa took one last picture in the preschool class—a lone yellow slicker hanging in the coat room, taken with a 20 mm wide-angle to emphasize the emptiness of the room—and then turned to Mrs. Yeh.

Throughout the long day, the Chinese woman had barely smiled and certainly not at Tessa. It happened that way sometimes, the imposition of Tessa on another's domain—unwelcome and unwanted.

And yet somewhere in Tessa's thirteen rolls of film were three shots that showed Mrs. Yeh's skill with the children: One, taken from behind Mrs. Yeh, showed the children gathered around her—rapt, attentive, eager—taking in every word she said. Another showed Mrs. Yeh patting a child's cheek, the boy serene under her gentle attention. And finally—Tessa's favorite—showed Mrs. Yeh at the Jurong Bird Park laughing as she tried to stretch a peek at the parrot on her head. By crouching down almost into the dirt, Tessa got this shot from a very low angle, catching the children's reaction to their teacher's uneasiness, and yet with the perspective showing Mrs. Yeh's stature among them.

She had bracketed the shot, taking a series at different settings. If even one worked as well as she hoped, she would submit it to her stock agency, which made her photographs available for general purchase, and the shot could make money for years to come.

"I had a wonderful day," Tessa told Mrs. Yeh now, "and you are a wonderful teacher. If I had children myself, I would be happy to bring them to your class." She paused, giving importance to the statement through silence, and then held out two bags of candies. "I brought these for your own children. I hope they enjoy them."

And at last there came a genuine smile for Tessa. "You took good pictures, I hope?"

"Yes, charming pictures that will bring honor to your school and to you. I will send you some of the best, okay?"

Mrs. Yeh nodded, and Tessa said good-bye.

Once outside she climbed into the taxi she had called for earlier and grinned at the driver as she spoke her destination. Children, sunshine, wildlife, and humor—what a great day. How could she ever give this up?

As for the evening ahead, she was eating with Ivy Tan, her Asia Premier editor. In her late twenties and still unmarried, Ivy Tan had short black hair and large oval-rimmed glasses, which together gave her a modern, stylish appearance. Sitting together the previous Saturday evening, she and Tessa had taken an immediate interest in each other and arranged to meet tonight.

It was almost six now. Tessa looked down at her clothes. The knees of her slacks were scuffed and grass-stained from all the kneeling she had done throughout the day, and the seat of her pants was probably dusty. If she needed to, she'd change after meeting Ivy.

At her office, Ivy shrugged off Tessa's appearance. "I feel like cooking anyway. Do you mind eating in?"

"Not at all."

A taxi took them east, to a group of high-rise buildings almost directly on the beach. After a stop at a nearby fruit and vegetable stand, Ivy took Tessa up to her apartment. There could be no doubt about its cost. The rooms faced the water and were high in the building, both sure signs of an extremely expensive price.

Inside, cool white and gray walls punctuated by Shoji screens and wooden flooring gave a serene background for the black marble surfaces, off-white furniture, and brilliant red flowers that decorated the room. Vivid and energetic herself, Ivy obviously desired a calm, contrasting background.

"This is beautiful," Tessa said.

Ivy laughed delightedly. "For which I must thank my father. He's an old-time businessman who has investments in everything from electronics to action figures. It's a sign of status to keep me so richly settled. Help yourself to drinks in the cabinet. I'm going to change my clothes. There's soda in the fridge as well."

Tessa went to the bookshelves first. Ivy's tastes ran in nonfiction and history primarily, with books on Asian mythology and anthropology mixed in. She subscribed to both Chinese and English magazines, including among others *The Economist, The New Yorker, Rolling Stone,* and a few scattered issues of *People.*

From there, remembering the drink, Tessa went to the kitchen. Though compact, it had every convenience. Tessa smoothed her hand over the handmade ceramic tiles above the counter. Ivy's father had spent plenty even on the details.

"Imported from Portugal," Ivy said from behind her. "Can you believe it?"

"Your father's very generous."

"Sure he is. But the way I see it, I'm doing him the favor, allowing the opportunity to show off his great success. This apartment is *obiangism* at its most flagrant, don't you think? Hey, no drink yet?"

"I'll take a Coke—yes, with ice, thank you. And no, I don't know what *obiangism* is."

Ivy poured herself some wine, then took the fresh foods out of her stretchy string bag: a cucumber, shallots, a thin yellow plant that looked like a green onion, and a handful of long, very thin green vegetables. "Have a seat on that stool there, while I cook."

As Tessa watched, Ivy finished with the first vegetables—asparagus beans, she called them—and began peeling and trimming the cucumber. She did so with such speed and precision that Tessa knew she had spent long hours cooking.

"It's a kind of art in itself," she said. "I genuinely love it. I could do it all day."

"And yet you've chosen a career."

Ivy halted her knife mid-stroke. "Chosen? Tessa, dear Tessa—where did you get the idea that modern Singapore offered choices? In modern Singapore a woman has to have it all—career, husband, children, and all of it perfect. I could no more marry and stay at home right now than…I don't know, than Singapore could give back all the land it's taken from the sea. Is it not the same in your America—a slight bias against bright, intelligent women who decide to leave their careers?"

"But the husband and children?"

"Postponed as long as possible. I'd rather stay single than enter that rat race."

She applied new vigor to her chopping, then deftly peeled and deveined five medium shrimp.

Tessa propped her elbows on the counter. "You were going to explain obiangism."

"I was, wasn't I? I just need to fry these shallots and put some rice in the cooker, then we can go out on the balcony. There's a nice breeze that comes up from the ocean, it's fairly cool. Hold on a minute."

As the shallots were frying, Ivy put the prepared vegetables and herbs into the refrigerator, pulled rice and a cooker from the cabinet, and returned to the frying pan in time to remove the shallots from the oil and replace them with the shrimp. A few quick movements, and the rice was cooking, in time to remove the shrimp from the frying pan.

"Come," she said, not even winded.

She plucked up her wine and led the way to the balcony, where an arrangement of potted plants, each around six feet high, spread their leafy branches. Ivy waved toward the outdoor furniture, clean and new, but went herself to the rail.

Tessa followed her. "Quite a view."

"Take a picture. The way the government's reclaiming land, in a few years we'll be a couple blocks inland, with another luxury housing development between us and the water."

As ironic as her words sounded, from the way Ivy held her face up to the breeze, from the deep relaxing breath she took, from the slow sigh of contentment, she did find great solace from the sea.

"Okay," she said, after settling herself into one of the chairs, "obiangism. Two ideas, actually, capture what being Chinese in Singapore is all about: kiasuism and obiangism. As simply as possible, obiangism means a conspicuous display of acquired wealth—the more ostentatious and gaudy and sensational the better. We do it to prove our success."

"But your apartment is very tasteful."

"Thank you, but I went to college and graduate school in the States. Perhaps it's a generational thing, or just the passage of time. You should have seen my parents' first home—Gothic pillars on a tiny row house with rococo revival furniture inside." She shuddered.

A faint *ping* sounded from inside the apartment, and Ivy stood. "That's the rice cooker. I'll be right back."

A few minutes later, she brought out a serving bowl with the rice, shrimp, and herbs tossed together and the cucumber, beans, and shallots scattered over the top. She set it on the patio table, then returned for place settings, which Tessa laid out.

"Delicious," Tessa said, after tasting the rice dish. "No wonder you like to cook."

"My mother would be appalled to think I was only serving you one dish, and a lowly one like *nasi ulam* at that—little more than rice with vegetables."

"Not quite *obiang* enough?"

"Come to my parents' house for cocktails Saturday night. You can see for yourself."

Tessa hesitated. "Perhaps another time? A friend might be stopping off this weekend on his way to an assignment in Singapore."

"Bring him along, and that banker cousin of yours for me—he's unattached, isn't he?—and we'll go out on the town together. Come on, don't keep them to yourself."

Tessa laughed. "I'll see if they're free. Are you sure your parents won't mind?"

"Of course not. They entertain on a grand scale, another tribute to Singaporean excess." She wagged her finger at Tessa. "If you refuse, it would cause a frightful loss of face."

"Then thank you, I accept. Saving face, unlike obiangism, is an Asian concept I'm quite familiar with."

"But Singapore is defined by more than just obiangism. If you want to understand being Chinese in Singapore, you need to understand kiasuism as well. We're all deathly afraid, you know, that someone will gain an advantage over us. That's why we almost kill each other getting onto a bus. And heaven forbid that someone else get a better seat in the theater or the best bargain at a department store sale or the table we want at a restaurant."

Tessa smiled. "I've seen some of the Mr. Kiasu comic strips in the *Straits Times*."

"Then you know, we never take anything for granted—and just as well, I think." Ivy lifted her wine glass toward the high-rises around them. "That national insecurity complex has pushed us far and very fast."

"I think you must be right," Tessa said.

In the long moments of stretching sunlight and gathering shadows of dusk following the meal, Tessa brought out her camera and played with the view from Ivy's balcony, shooting a few lazy shots of Ivy herself. Tessa had enjoyed her company. Though Ivy had been blunt in her criticism, mocking the Chinese people's habits, Tessa suspected she wouldn't ever want to live anywhere else—a true Singaporean.

Tessa got up early the next day, before five. She wanted to be on Serangoon Street in time to catch the merchants setting up their shops and market stalls. She'd stay through the morning—shoppers always provided colorful possibilities, and when the sun overhead became too harsh for good pictures, she'd retreat inside some of the bigger stores.

Before leaving, she sat at the kitchen table with a mug of coffee and jotted down photo possibilities. She'd take a whole series on Indian women—the flowers in their hair, close-ups of their jewelry, details on their saris. The artisans would be interesting, perhaps taken at very slow speed to give a sense of how quiet and dark their shops were. She kept adding ideas until she had ten or twelve to start with, then rose and hefted her photo bag onto her shoulder.

If she didn't get enough for a travel essay, she might at least be able to send some shots to the stock agency. No day was ever completely wasted.

She returned to Jillian's apartment shortly before three in the afternoon, feeling exhausted, gritty, and pleased with what she had on film. She would have to go again, probably twice more, especially for twilight and the early evening hours. The smaller shops that opened onto the streets yielded colorful shots of merchants pulling out their wares from the dark interiors of the shops and arranging them for display. Tomorrow she might go back and ask permission to shoot from inside one of the large sari shops, and even get some pictures of the lodging provided on the upper floors for itinerant laborers from India. Or perhaps on Saturday she would get more pictures of children. They seemed to be strangely absent, at least during the week.

Before doing anything else, she checked the labeling on her rolls of film, cross-checked them with her log book, and then loaded them into Jillian's freezer. She'd have to locate a reputable studio soon to have her film developed—that or send the film stateside. At some point, too, she should check and repack her equipment, then transfer her caption notes to disk.

But first a shower.

On the way to her bedroom, she found a note from Jillian on the door: *Call Michael at work.*

Tessa stared down at the slip of paper. A few more encounters like the one Tuesday evening and that portion of her mission in Singapore would be over. He'd been irritated to have her show up unannounced, and not in the least pleased to help her get that picture from the roof. She was sure of it. So what did he want now?

She crumpled the paper in her hand. She'd take her shower first and then call him. She stepped closer to the wastepaper basket, took aim, and fired.

There you go, Michael Lawton.

Feeling refreshed, she emerged from the bathroom clad only in her robe. Jillian wasn't likely to show up at four in the afternoon with another new conquest. Tessa finished her computer backup and equipment check, got herself a soft drink, and opened up the *Straits Times*.

Only then did she allow herself to punch in Michael's automatic dial number at Chadsworth.

"Ah, good," he said. "I thought I would miss you."

No hint of restraint in his voice now.

"Did you want something?" She purposely put a little drawl in her voice and rustled the newspaper page so he'd hear that as well.

Cool as ever, he continued without missing a beat. "I have a soccer game at six this evening. If you'd like to come by the field, afterward we could eat some of that Nonya food my housemaid makes for me."

She pressed her lips together and let the silence lengthen.

"Tessa? Can you come? I don't have much time."

He seldom did, apparently. She glanced at her watch. She had never seen where he lived. She admitted to a little aesthetic curiosity—an artistic sentiment, nothing more.

"Where exactly is your game?"

"Write the name of this park down." He spelled it out for her and had her practice saying the Chinese name. "You'll need to call ahead for a taxi. Here's the company I use. Will that be okay?"

She could sense his need to get away.

"I'll be fine."

"Just in case, here's my cell phone number. Call if necessary."

She turned the collar of her robe up and wrapped it around her neck. A soccer game would be fun, more fun than e-mailing her photo-rep about the Serangoon Street project. Why not? She'd take her camera to the park, maybe even catch some pictures of Singaporean families relaxing together after work.

Besides, she had to ask Michael about Corin staying over, didn't she?

EIGHT

Tessa took her time dressing, knowing all the time that she was stalling in order to send Michael a not-too-subtle message. She tried on three outfits from her limited supply before settling on a periwinkle print jumper over a small white tee. She loved the freedom of wearing sandals, not always an option in her more primitive locations, and only hoped the soccer field wouldn't be scratchy or uncomfortable on her nearly bare feet.

She arrived at 6:15 and wondered if she had come to the right place. The park, with one massive green area, had been divided into ten or twelve fields, and all had children playing on them.

Children?

They seemed to be of all nationalities, and many different ages.

She walked toward the first field and looked around. When she didn't see Michael, she walked on toward the next one. Finally, coming toward the far corner, she heard a loud whistle, checked where it came from, and stopped in her tracks.

Michael stood about two-thirds of the way down the field, surrounded—literally pressed in on every side—by a dozen or more preschoolers. He pointed toward one of the children, the referee set the ball down, and play resumed, Michael and a woman running alongside the children as they chased the ball downfield.

Tessa groped for her camera. Michael Lawton, coaching preschool soccer. He looked at home, laughing, smoothing a little boy's hair back, giving instructions, grinning again.

If she'd ever needed proof that his life had gone on without her, here it was.

One of the players—one of *Michael's* players—headed off with the ball in the wrong direction, bringing a chorus of instructions from the sideline and a fast sprint from Michael. Alongside the intensely focused little girl, he waved her back. Unfortunately a boy from the other team snagged the ball from under her feet, kept it going toward the goal, and scored. The little girl burst into tears. Michael picked her up and hugged her, brown curly hair buried close against his shoulder.

A small sound escaped from Tessa.

Michael said something, and the little girl nodded reluctantly, lower lip out, then nodded again. Michael set her on the ground, and she ran off, much happier, to take the goalie's place.

Tessa walked closer, and Michael saw her. "We just started," he shouted, trying to keep one eye on the children. "Have a seat."

A row of faces on the near sideline turned in her direction, parents of Michael's players perhaps, and one of the women beckoned toward a vacant lawnchair. "Over here," she said. Around forty, overweight but very pretty, she gave Tessa a friendly smile. "You must be Michael's cousin. I'm Carol de Vos. My husband Gary is the other coach standing down by the goal."

Tessa took the vacant chair, and Carol introduced some of the other people close by, many of whom went to the same church Michael did. After some obvious curiosity, they settled back to watch the game again.

Tessa had never seen a game like this one. Everything seemed small—the children, the field, even the goal, which was so small the little girl could almost touch both posts by stretching out her arms.

"I'm surprised they ever score," Tessa said, "the goal's so small."

Carol laughed. "You wait. These younger kids get so easily distracted. That's why Gary's down there—to warn the goalie when the ball starts coming her way."

"And Michael?"

"He runs alongside to coach them on the field."

The children all bunched around the ball, like iron filings to a magnet, until one of the children broke free and dribbled in spurts toward a goal, the other children stumbling along behind.

And there was Michael, unfailingly watchful, running along with them.

"I can't believe he's doing this," Tessa said, more to herself than to Carol.

"Our fault, I'm afraid," she said. "The red-haired boy over there—yes, the one charging down the field with the ball—he's our youngest. This league is run by ANZA—the Australian New Zealand Association. When they asked Gary about coaching, he roped Michael in."

The ref blew his whistle, and play stopped.

"Substitutions," Carol said.

Michael came toward the sidelines, motioned for replacements and gave instructions, finding time in the process to smile at Tessa.

She searched her mind for something to say, but all she could think was how good he looked out there, how right holding a child in his arms, how lucky the kids were to have him. But she couldn't *say* any of that!

So she just wrinkled her nose at him and grinned.

Play resumed, and Tessa took out a camera and fixed a 35-75 mm zoom lens on it. She had come prepared with some

400 ISO film. The low, warm sunlight would be perfect, with the green grass and vivid yellow uniforms providing wonderfully saturated colors. Of course, the picture she really wanted she had already missed: Michael comforting the little dark-haired girl.

And what would you do with it? Frame it and weep?

Tessa slung her bag over her shoulders, her habit of protecting her equipment too ingrained for her to consider leaving anything for Carol to guard, and began walking around the field, checking out angles and perspectives. She took a few frames, but decided her best hope for good pictures would be at halftime, close in, with a 28 mm lens.

"Michael mentioned you were a photographer," Carol said, once Tessa had taken a seat again.

"But not usually sports."

"What, then?"

"Travel photography, some industry shots for business publications, mostly in Asia, but anywhere people will pay me. A little photojournalism."

"Is sports a lot harder?"

"No, not harder. Just different." Carol seemed interested, so Tessa continued. "Part of what I do is anticipate a picture opportunity before it happens so that I'm set up to get the best angle, the right light, the most workable background, all at just the right time. That takes a lot of practice and a huge dose of intuition. I don't watch enough sports to do it well." Tessa nodded her head toward the field and smiled. "Though even I'm beginning to figure out what's going on out there."

Carol laughed. "With our team, not much soccer! But who cares? Some of these parents are incredibly serious, but for us, at this age, it's mostly about fun. Oh, look. It's halftime."

"Glad you could make it," Michael said when he came over.

He pulled a cooler from behind a nearby lawn chair. "Fruit juice?"

"If you have enough."

He handed her a bottle, then sat on the ground in front of her, lifting his face to hers. It was a perfect pose. Against the grass around him, the blue in his eyes appeared more vivid than the sky, his smile brighter than the sun. She lifed her camera.

"More good lighting?" He looked quite pleased with himself—as if he knew exactly what subject she'd like to catch.

"It's the children," she said. "They're wonderful."

He laughed. "Yes, they are, aren't they?" He looked down the near sideline of the soccer field. "I can't wait. In fact—" He caught himself, frowned down at his juice bottle, and cleared his throat. "Anyway, I'm glad you're enjoying yourself."

But Tessa was following his gaze down the sidelines to the fathers, mothers, and children nearby. She knew what he was thinking. He was ready for some of his own, that's what it was. He'd been eager for children four years ago as well, but with his desire came strong convictions about what children needed in a family, and a mother who traveled for months at a time wasn't on the list. He'd made that very clear.

She set her bottle down, unable to drink anymore.

The whistle blew. Michael stuffed his empty bottle into the cooler and jumped to his feet. "Back to work." He paused, looking down at her. "I'll see you afterward?"

Tessa nodded.

During the second half, Carol de Vos unwittingly added to Tessa's tension. "About Michael..." She pulled her chair closer. "Can you tell me—you're his cousin, so you must know—does he ever talk about Angie Buckley? Does he keep in touch with her?"

"I—I don't know."

"They went out together for a while last year. We thought for sure something would come of it—I can't believe he's not married—but then Angie was called away to the home office—she's with the Navigators like we are—and that was the last we heard of it." Carol frowned. "You really don't know?"

"Sorry."

"Maybe I'll drop her a line. Then there's this woman at the bank, what about her? Jill, I think her name is."

"Jillian," Tessa said.

"So you do know about her? What do you think? Any chance there?"

"Michael and I haven't seen each other in years," Tessa said. "You should ask him."

"Oh, too bad. Believe me, I've tried to get Gary to find out, but you know how guys are." Carol rolled her eyes. "Anyway, that's why he's transferring back to the States this summer. I'm sure of it. More chance of finding a wife on his home turf." She shook her head. "It's a shame."

To Tessa's relief, Carol turned her attention back to the game. Unwilling to face any more questions, Tessa stood and walked the sidelines but with neither the energy nor the desire to lift her Nikon for a picture. She did manage a quick picture as Michael came off the field.

"Are you Moses out there?" she said. "Or the Pied Piper?"

He laughed. "More like Gulliver about to be toppled by the Lilliputians."

And then, with almost a single motion, he stripped away his sweaty T-shirt, rubbed it across his chest, and replaced it with a clean one from his duffel bag.

Tessa blinked. Whoa. As if she wasn't confused enough already.

"Hey," someone said from behind Michael, "you must be

Tessa. I'm Gary de Vos. Nice of you to come to the game."

"How about joining us for dinner?" Carol said. "We're going to round up the rest of our kids and head over to Pizza Hut. They'll be finished in about twenty minutes."

Tessa glanced around. "They're playing in other games? How many do you have?"

"Three others, all boys: seven, ten, and thirteen."

Michael turned to Tessa. "What do you think? I can save Mrs. Ling's food for later."

Tessa nodded. "Okay."

"Why don't we meet you there in thirty minutes?" Michael said. "Order me anything except mushrooms. As for Tessa—" He glanced her way and grinned. "She'll eat anything."

Tessa planted a fist on her hip, ready to protest, but when she lifted scolding eyes to his, found she couldn't speak. There was something in his eyes, warmth or hope or maybe even longing—she couldn't say for sure—but she hadn't seen it in any man's eyes except Michael's, and not even in his for four long years.

She heard Gary say something behind her, she thought perhaps a question, but she couldn't pull her gaze from Michael's

It was like slipping on ice, everything normal, then a sudden, dizzying skid, and no idea where she'd end up.

He must have seen the panic. His hand lifted, but she knew—if he touched her— How could she survive?

In desperation she spun around to face Gary. "Yes. Even anchovies." She shook her head. "Though I don't really like them."

"Come on," Michael said. "Our taxi's waiting." He swept up his duffel bag over one shoulder, hefted the cooler with the same arm, and gestured toward the road. "This way." To the de Voses he said, "We'll see you there."

In the taxi, after one glance in her direction, he wiped a towel across his still sweaty forehead, draped it around his neck, then sat back and let the ride pass in silence. And yet in that one glance she thought she'd seen a smile, if not on his lips, in his eyes.

What did that mean?

And why would it make her so nervous?

In his apartment, to her relief, he immediately excused himself, leaving her free to explore his living room. It was quintessentially Michael. A bank of shelves, crowded with books. Modern artwork, certainly original, and offbeat sculptures on the end tables. An entertainment unit stocked with brands so expensive Tessa didn't even recognize them, and fresh-cut flowers everywhere.

The books interested her the most. On the shelves she found Asian history, politics, sociology, along with some Tom Clancy, John Grisham, and a row of theology. When he came out, she was looking at a book on apologetics by Ravi Zacharias.

"Heard of him?"

"Yes, I have, though I haven't read this book."

"I use it for a Bible study I teach." His voice was calm, his expression relaxed. She wondered if she'd imagined the tension in the taxi.

"Is that the study you teach on Wednesday nights?"

He nodded. "You probably realize by now, people in Singapore take as dogma the 'same God' idea—different beliefs, different practices, different names, but all the same God. I was amazed at how many people who call themselves Christians accept this, so I decided to teach a class on why, logically, Christian belief is too distinctive to allow the 'same God' idea."

"Which falls under apologetics."

"Exactly." He held a hand out toward the door. "Ready to go?"

In the elevator, hoping to keep the conversation neutral, she asked about Tuesday night. "You were going to a meeting."

"A business dinner with some executives from a small petrochemical company. They're hoping to restructure their loan so they can expand."

"And you're helping them?"

"I'm doing the calculations, yes."

She leaned against the wall of the elevator. "Is it hard, what you do?"

"The challenge is maintaining our profit while keeping their payments low enough. That means figuring in assets and projected earnings, proper deferrals, and a whole lot more. It's like a giant puzzle where the pieces keep changing shape."

"It sounds like more creative thinking than people give bankers credit for."

He grinned. "Thanks...I think." As she passed him getting out of the elevator, he said, "By the way, tomorrow I'm going out to tour their plant on one of the Jurong Islands. Would you like to come with me?"

Tessa stopped where she was. "A chemical plant? I'd love to."

"Great."

"No, really," she said, after they had climbed into a taxi. "Industry shots, especially foreign ones, keep up a steady sale in stock photography."

"Stock photography?"

"I submit photos to an agency in New York. It offers the pictures for lease to whoever wants them."

"Do you get many takers?"

She hesitated. The idea had been to make *him* talk.

"Tessa?"

"Not as many as I'd like. I'm never quite sure what will appeal to the people who use stock agencies—textbook companies, ad agencies, anyone who wants to skip the cost of location shooting. I specialize in pictures of people, especially in ethnic dress, but the ones that sell the best have some kind of added dimension. They're funny or poignant or show emotion in some other way."

"So I could open *Time* or *Newsweek* and see one of your pictures in an advertisement?"

"My biggest moneymaker isn't even a travel shot. I was with my stepmother, Jenny, one day. She was driving. I happened to glance back at a stop light. In the car behind us, the husband was looking to his left, the wife to her right—both lost in their own thoughts. If Jenny's car hadn't had a sun roof, I wouldn't have tried it, but I managed to open the window, get up on the seat, and take several pictures before the light changed."

"Poor Jenny."

"Oh, she didn't mind the gymnastics as much as chasing the car down afterwards to get model releases. Stock agencies insist on signed releases."

"But that photo's made you a lot of money?"

"Maybe $40,000 to date. Psychology textbooks, marriage manuals, anything related to communication—somehow the picture captures visually what a lot of authors want to say."

"Interesting."

They had arrived at Pizza Hut. Tessa climbed out after Michael, then waited as he paid. "In fact," she began, then paused. She had been talking too much.

"Yes?"

Why not? "I think I may have gotten another good stock photo on Wednesday. My editor here, Ivy Tan, arranged for me to spend the day at a preschool." She described the photo with the parrot.

"I'd like to see it," he said. "When will you have a copy?"

"I'm not sure. If I get it developed before I leave, I'll let you know."

"You mean leave Singapore." A large group pushed past them into the restaurant. He didn't seem in any hurry to follow them in. "What's next, after this?"

"Bombay—oops." She shook her head. "I keep forgetting they've changed the name. Mumbai. I'll be photographing executives for an annual report. The previous photographer had to cancel, but it's so straightforward, and it fits so nicely between this one and my next longer assignment. I couldn't turn it down."

"And what's that one—the longer one, I mean?"

"Shouldn't we go in, Michael?"

"In a minute. Tell me about the assignment first."

She swallowed. "It's in Australia, at a hospital in Alice Springs, photographing aborigines. That'll be hard. They're notoriously shy of cameras. But most people don't realize how desperately in need of medical care the outback people are. It seems worth the effort."

"Sounds suspiciously like photojournalism."

"I'm hoping to find one young girl who's about to have her baby—so many get pregnant at twelve and thirteen—and do a photo essay on her." She glanced at her watch. "Michael, it's been forty minutes already. They'll be wondering where we are."

"Okay. Sure." He pushed open the door. "You can tell me more later."

~ ~ ~ ~ ~

The interior of the restaurant looked so much like a Pizza Hut in America that Tessa had to pinch herself. The de Voses, all six of them, waited at a table near the corner. Only the youngest, Davy, had red hair. The others had their parents' light brown hair. All had masses of freckles, quick smiles, huge appetites, and an obvious affection for Michael. Davy and the next youngest, Nate, won the right to sit beside him, leaving Tessa halfway around the table next to Carol.

The noisy meal offered an interesting comparison to the happy hour at Harry's the Friday before. There, young professionals, comfortable in their wealth, seemed happy to insulate themselves in an expatriate haven. Here a missionary family, limited financially, was doing its best to fit into Singaporean society at large. It showed in the way Gary and Carol related to the waitress. Carol smiled and spoke politely, and Gary struck up a conversation with the young woman, joking about his crew of pizza monsters.

And what of Michael, who could claim the status of money and respected financial profession? Anyone watching, without knowing them, would assume Michael was Gary's younger brother.

Only Tessa felt outside the family loop, the visitor again, who needed names repeated, jokes explained, who received only shy smiles from the children and none of the comfortable exchange of unspoken messages so common among friends.

For Tessa's benefit Gary described how he and Carol had met in ninth-grade homeroom. "I knew two weeks into the semester she was the only one for me." He gave Carol a warm smile. "It happens that way sometimes. You meet someone and that's it. No one else will do."

Tessa had her hand halfway to her mouth. She let it drop to

the table. Sometimes? Yes. But not *always*. Surely not always.

"You guys have probably known each other all your lives," Carol said.

Michael, too, had set his pizza down. "No." His eyes met Tessa's for a sensitive moment, and he gave her a sad smile. "We met ten years ago, actually. She was staying with her mother in Japan after graduating from high school. I had just graduated from college myself, and my parents decided it would be a good time for me to see a little of the world. Naturally I stopped to visit my uncle."

"Her mother; your uncle?" Carol shook her head. "I don't understand."

Michael explained.

"You mean...you're not really related?"

"No." Michael ruffled Davy's hair. "Not that I would have minded knowing Tessa at this age." He glanced again in Tessa's direction.

He was making his regret over their past breakup obvious, but what did that mean for now? Was he forgetting why it hadn't worked out all those years ago?

Carol was nodding, slowly "No wonder you don't see each other very often."

"Not often in the last four years," Michael agreed. "But maybe we'll do better from now on. What do you think, Tessa? Can we do better...this time?"

She could hardly breathe. That he should say this now, in the presence of witnesses. That he should ask so seriously.

"Sure," she managed, determined to miss his real question. "Why not?"

NINE

S omething wrong?" Michael said outside after they had seen the de Voses off.

"Not a thing," Tessa said, lying through her teeth.

An intermittent breeze swept through the street, providing a little relief to Tessa's reddened cheeks. Even on a Thursday night, people crowded the sidewalks. She hesitated, bracing herself for whatever was coming, but he didn't seem in a hurry to follow up on his question.

"What now?" she said.

"Would you like to walk a little way?"

"It's getting late."

"Then let's at least walk a ways toward home." He held a hand out in the right direction, and she set off, grateful to be walking beside him, freed from eye contact.

She forced a cheerful voice. "They're a nice family, Michael. Are you happy Gary convinced you to help coach?"

"It provides a wonderful balance to the rest of the week."

"A little different from last Friday at Harry's, that's for sure. What a very adaptable person you are, Michael. Is there any group of people you can't fit in with?"

"Some people certainly." His voice sounded different. He had slowed his steps, forcing her to as well, and when she glanced up at him, there it was again, that hope and longing, with concern mixed in this time as well. "Like Tuesday, on the roof, Tessa. I'm sorry I—"

His cell phone interrupted him. He let out a long breath, then grunted apologetically and pulled it out of his side pocket. "Michael Lawton here." His expression altered. "Jillian! What's the matter?" He frowned. "Easy now. Slow down." He listened a moment longer, then sucked in his breath. "You're sure? When was that?" He pushed a hand across his forehead and groaned. "Yes. Okay." His voice became very gentle, almost tender, and he lifted his other hand to the receiver, as if it were Jillian herself he was touching. "Hold on, Jillian. Yes. Take it easy. I'm coming."

He stood looking down at the phone for a long minute. Then he lifted his face, still stunned, to Tessa.

"I'm sorry. Something's come up." He was already calling for a taxi.

"At the bank?" she said when he was finished.

"I'll take you back to her place before I go."

"She's not at home?"

"No."

"I can make it on my own."

"No. I'll come."

He didn't speak during the short taxi ride, but at the door to her building, he apologized again. "Not quite the way I intended the evening to end, I'm afraid."

Cryptic, but she didn't want to know what he meant. "It's okay. Don't worry about it."

She did want to ask about the emergency. He hadn't confirmed that Jillian called from the bank, though since she wasn't at home, she must have. It would make sense that she'd call Michael with a problem at work.

"I'll pick you up tomorrow at eight-thirty," Michael was saying, "for that tour of the chemical plant. Dress comfortably but nice, since it will be an executive tour. Until then, have a good evening."

And then, against all expectations, he leaned forward and pressed a light kiss against her forehead. He paused, his body so close, then drew back and shook his head. "I better get going."

"Wait!" she said.

Michael was already walking away. Tessa hurried after him.

"I forgot to ask you. A friend, Corin Bolt, another photographer—he's stopping by this weekend on the way to a shoot in Indonesia. Could you put him up, do you think?"

"You mean, at the apartment?"

"You have an extra bedroom, don't you? He thought since we were cousins, you wouldn't mind. You know how expensive hotels are."

"When is he coming?"

"Saturday afternoon, which brings up something else. I, um, my editor, Ivy Tan, asked about bringing you to cocktails at her parents' house on Saturday evening. He's a big industrialist—"

"Tan Lee Ying?"

"Yes. That's his name. She mentioned going out somewhere together afterwards."

"And Corin," Michael said. "Will he be coming, too?"

"Yes, a foursome. That's what she thought."

"I'll have to let you know."

"I could ask Jillian about letting Corin bunk on her couch if you'd rather."

"No!" The word shot out of him. He must have seen her surprise. "It's not a good weekend for anyone to stay at Jillian's. Don't worry. I'll put your friend up."

Behind her carefully blank face, her mind raced with questions. "Thank you, Michael. Corin will leave Sunday sometime."

"Fine. Now I have to go. I'll see you tomorrow."

~ ~ ~ ~ ~

Tessa stepped into Jillian's apartment. Empty as expected. But if the problem was at the bank, why hadn't he told her?

She called Corin, intending to tell him Michael had agreed to put him up. His machine answered, and she left a message instead. "Call me," she said before hanging up.

Corin would come with or without her invitation. Just as well. Perhaps seeing him would remind her why she had chosen photography four years ago.

Yet no wonder after this evening she was confused. Michael so perfectly fit what she wanted in a man—it was all coming back to her—and if those smiles were anything to judge by, he was still attracted to her as well. She pressed cooling palms to her cheeks. Best of all, he'd be unfailingly faithful to any marriage he entered and committed without faltering to Jesus Christ as well.

But that was the problem. *He'd expect you to be equally committed, to the marriage and to his idea of what God wants, even to the point of giving up your call.*

She prepared for bed, read her habitual three chapters from the Bible, worked on the next psalm she was memorizing, then flipped off her bedside lamp. Ten o'clock. Whatever they were doing they were still at it. Jillian still hadn't returned.

What were they doing?

She rearranged her pillows, found what she thought was a comfortable position, and closed her eyes.

And why was this a bad weekend for company?

She opened her eyes.

Was Jillian going to be at the bank, working late hours, possibly through the night? Was that why?

Surely Michael wasn't worried about Tessa being alone at the apartment with Corin. Michael, after all, knew nothing yet about Corin, his age or good looks, his confident appeal to women. No. There must be something else to make this a bad weekend.

And that kiss…

She flipped over to her other side. Not a warm glass of milk, that kiss. No kiss from Michael ever could be. She punched her pillow. What was he thinking?

She turned over again. Her legs ached. She must have strained them that morning on Serangoon Street, squatting for so long, waiting for the woman in the scarlet sari to turn from her business. *That* was why she was having such a hard time getting to sleep.

Not at all the feel of his hand gripping her shoulder, the image of blue eyes so close, the shock of warm lips against her skin.

And not the memory of her instinctive lunge forward, either.

Had he noticed?

She groaned and tried the other side again. It was so brief, that contact, nothing more than a sign of friendship, a polite good night.

But he *had* said "not how he intended the evening to end"…

She flopped over onto her back and stared at the shadowed ceiling above. On other nights like this, on a hard ground, muscles weary from work, edged with worry over her pictures, she began at the beginning of Psalms and recited each one that she knew—Psalm 1, Psalm 2, Psalm 8—the list included thirteen at the moment. Almost invariably, the familiar words calmed her mind so she could sleep. But starting the recitation always proved hardest, and tonight was no exception.

She flipped to her left side again and grinned into the darkness. Tonight she had Michael to think about. Michael, who had never done more than kiss her, even when they were engaged; who had never invited her, as Corin had, to join him in bed. Who, even without asking, made her imagine—

She turned to her right side and started forcing the words through gritted teeth: "Blessed is the man who does not walk in the counsel of the wicked...."

She had progressed to the first verses of Psalm 139 when she heard the apartment door open, Michael's voice a soft murmur and Jillian's response. The door shut, and Jillian moved toward her bedroom. Then quiet again.

Twelve-thirty.

Tessa turned over more slowly. This time she had to get some sleep.

Michael showed no signs of his late night when he arrived the next morning. "Good," he said, after checking out her linen slacks and matching buttoned vest. "And no hat today, I see."

"They'll issue hard hats, I'm sure."

"Yes, of course. You've done this before."

She watched him closely as he held the door open for her. Not a hint of explanation for last night.

"Tell me what I'll see this morning."

"We're heading toward one of the Jurong Islands, a huge reclamation project that will add five thousand acres of land from the sea—all of it designated for chemical companies. The government is linking seven already existing islands and adding substantially to them. By the time they're done, sometime around 2007, Jurong Island will represent about five percent of Singapore's total land mass."

"And the company we're touring?"

"Hang Petrochemicals. They produce ethylene and propylene, used mainly in producing plastics. The board of directors wants to take advantage of government support for expansion. That's why they're asking for a bigger loan."

"And they came to you rather than an Asian bank?"

"I arranged their first loan three years ago."

"But if you're that well acquainted with the company, why go out and tour their facilities now?"

He frowned.

"You don't mind these questions, do you?"

"No, not at all. You're just not the first person who has wondered about my hands-on approach. I'm probably risking offense by being so cautious, but better to find out about problems before the fact rather than afterward." He shrugged. "The way I see it, the banking business takes too much on faith. And even when they do discover fraud, they usually absorb the cost rather than go public with the crime. Fraud smacks of mismanagement and unsettles investors, and they can't risk that." He gave a rueful smile. "I've heard it said, in fact, that a top executive risks less stealing millions than a mail clerk risks stealing stamps. The executive gets a severance package; the mail clerk gets fired."

"That's horrible."

"What's a couple million to a bank like Chadsworth? If investors lose faith, the entire company could go under."

"So in the meantime, you keep checking?"

"Yes. This morning I'm seeing for myself that Hang Petrochemicals has maintained its facilities as they've said."

The plant edged the water by only a few feet, concrete slabs forming a wall along the beachfront. A cluster of holding tanks and off-white cylinders towered toward the sky, linked by extensive piping and scaffolding. Their Asian guide, Mr. Lee, scrutinized Tessa, making her realize Michael had stretched his influence by bringing her along. But in true Asian fashion he was unfailingly polite to her throughout the visit.

Her desire as a photographer was to balance man and machine, using size and perspective, camera angle and composition to highlight the human role in industry. She spent most of the morning close to Michael and Mr. Lee, climbing nearby stairs for better composition, ducking around or under tanks to get the right perspective, dropping further back to get a wider angle. Early on, Mr. Lee became alarmed when she looked as if she was going to climb some scaffolding to get above a worker checking valves. He sent for another worker to keep an eye on her, but Tessa had been in enough plants to know what would be allowed and what wouldn't be. Her biggest problem, as usual, was getting signed releases from all her subjects. When she and Michael left the plant shortly before noon, she had three rolls of usable film.

"Thank you," she told Michael in the taxi.

He looked up from the notes he was entering into his laptop. "Did it work out well for you? I was a little worried that the sky was too overcast."

"No, not at all. If anything, bright sun would have ruined my chances—glare and deep shadows."

He blinked. "So I should take most of my pictures on gray days? That seems strange."

"Or early in the morning or late afternoon. That light works well."

He nodded, smiled, then returned to his work. She sat back in her corner and watched him surreptitiously. She had been close enough during the morning to hear some of his conversation with Mr. Lee and came away impressed as always at his wide-ranging knowledge and smooth manner of dealing with people. That rich, preppy background, she thought wryly, but she also knew that Michael added character and integrity to whatever other privileges he had enjoyed.

"Lunch?" she said as they neared the downtown area. "I'm meeting with your pastor at two to ask about taking pictures during children's church, and to see if he can give me contacts for other opportunities next week, but there's plenty of time to stop somewhere."

He glanced at his watch. "Not today, I'm sorry. There's something I have to check on back at the office. But I'll see you tonight at Harry's, won't I? We're celebrating Blake's third million in loans."

"Is he really that good?"

"He's fast, that's for sure."

"Jillian thinks he's a snake."

He grunted. "She has strong opinions. While I don't find much to like in him myself, he's okay at the bank, and that's good enough for me. Anyway, about tonight. Around five-thirty?"

"I know I've seen him somewhere," she said.

"Yes?"

"I can't remember where, but he makes me very nervous." Michael was frowning. She could see she wasn't convincing him. "Jillian's right, Michael. He's dangerous somehow."

"Do you have a reason for thinking this?"

She scowled. "Let me figure out where I've seen him, and it'll probably make sense. As for tonight, five-thirty's fine."

He sighed. "I can try to track down his résumé, if you want, find out where he's lived."

"That might help. But, really, I'm probably making too much of it." She smiled. "You're a swinging bunch, for bankers. Happy hour two weeks in a row."

He grinned. "You have no idea. Harry's fills up every night. It's these ties." He pulled on his collar and gagged. "They cut off the oxygen."

"And sense with it? I'll remember that tonight." She wagged a finger at him. "Better behave."

After looking at her portfolio, Pastor Keenan agreed to her requests, offering other activities within the church if she needed them. She asked instead about native ministries. "I know there are Tamil Christian churches. Could you give me the name of a pastor I can call?"

"I certainly can." He pulled out his Rolodex and started flipping through. "Ready to take down these names?"

"You don't mind if I take a few pictures now, do you?"

He smoothed his unruly hair back and straightened his shirt. "Be my guest, though good luck with this nose."

He gave her the name of a Tamil pastor—"almost half the Indians in Singapore claim to be Christians, you know"—several Chinese names, and a contact with a drama ministry on campus. "That should give you some good photo opportunities," Pastor Keenan said, getting excited. "And you might want to check out some of the mission agencies that have training facilities here—Navigators, Overseas Missionary Fellowship, the Bethany School of Missions, to name a few. We're the Antioch of Asia, you know, a major base for international Christian organizations. Oh! I know…"

He flipped through his Rolodex. "Here's the name of a young man in our church who leads a Bible study for medical students. The more educated a person is in Singapore, the more likely they are to know Christ. Thirty percent of high school graduates are Christians, forty percent of college graduates, and medical students—they top the chart with seventy percent. Paul would be a good contact for you. And I have a good friend with the Navigators who has a ministry to the armed forces."

By the end, Tessa had a hard time stopping him. She had only a limited amount of time, and wanted most of all to take pictures of native Christians worshipping and ministering in uniquely Singaporean ways.

"Glad to help," Pastor Keenan said at the church door. "You know how it is: any friend of a friend."

"You mean Michael."

"We're going to miss him when he goes back to the States. New Christians in Singapore struggle constantly with the demands of affluence and the privileges it brings, and when expatriate Christians come in and assume that wealth and education automatically confer authority, it confuses the issue even more. Michael is one of the rare exceptions who never seems to lose sight of his role as steward, and his willingness to serve in the church and submit to leadership has provided a tremendous example to our community."

Tessa found that she had pressed a hand to her chest—her heart felt ready to burst. She touched Pastor Keenan's arm—a poor substitute for the hug she longed to give him. "Thank you so much. You've given me some wonderful leads."

"See you Sunday, then."

Using Pastor Keenan's name, Tessa spoke to the Tamil pastor and the coordinator for the drama troupe, then left messages for one of the migrant ministries and for the medical student.

She'd have a busy week, if all these leads worked out, but her first order of business on Monday morning would be to find that studio. She'd be needing more film soon. Ivy Tan could help.

When Tessa arrived at Harry's, only four people sat around the half-empty table. Gus stood and pulled back the chair on his right. Violet sat on his left, with Nigel and Blake across the table.

Blake didn't look at all pleased to see her. He glanced at his watch, shifted his gaze to the door. Was he planning his escape? Too bad the party was for him. He'd have to stay a few minutes.

And yet why this compulsion to get away? From what Jillian said, Blake enjoyed going in for the kill. If so, as much as he disliked her, why leave now?

"Michael had an errand," Violet said. "He'll be here any minute."

Gus waggled his eyebrows. "He wanted us to be sure and tell you."

"And Jillian?"

Violet shook her head. "She left work at lunch. She seemed quite upset about something."

"No wonder," Blake said. "She wouldn't be likely to celebrate my success now, would she?"

"Stuff it," Gus shot back.

Blake thrust his face across the table toward Gus, giving Tessa her first clear vision of his profile. "Are y'all telling me it doesn't bother her, me reaching three million so quickly, with her own record so much worse?"

"And are you *all* telling me you actually checked her record?" Gus said. "What's your problem, Bubba? You *all* are supposed to be working together, didn't you know that, not competing the whole time."

"You are nowhere near so naive." Alerted to Tessa's presence, perhaps by some small movement on her part, Blake glanced at her briefly, then pushed his chair back and stood up.

"I'm going to get some fresh air."

There he went again. Fear, not aversion, caused a man to flee, and yet why would he be afraid of her? She *must* know something about him, some incriminating piece of evidence. If only she could recognize him.

Tonight, she vowed, before the evening ended, she had to get a picture of him.

"Well, then," Gus said, turning to Tessa. "What have you been doing all week?"

Realizing her role, Tessa launched into an animated description of her activities. They enjoyed hearing about Ivy and added their own examples of obiangism and the kiasu mentality.

"Then this morning," Tessa concluded, "Michael offered me a tour of the Hang Petrochemicals plant. I spent the afternoon catching up on business—transferring caption notes to my computer files, mostly."

"A petrochemicals plant?" Violet scrunched up her nose. "That doesn't sound very photogenic."

"Ah, but very lucrative," Tessa responded. "Besides the sociological aspect—man's relationship to machine, there are all the trade journals and textbooks and business magazines that use photos like the ones I took this morning."

"And Michael offered this?" Nigel said. "He must have known you'd want to go."

Tessa blinked. "Yes, I think you're right."

How strange. She hadn't said anything about the kind of places she wanted to visit, only the kind of guides she preferred. And yet twice he had set up appointments rich with opportunities for her. The temple anyone might have predicted. How had he known about the value of taking pictures at a chemical plant?

Someone from a neighboring table came over, joking with Gus about something that had happened at SIMEX earlier that morning. Tessa slipped away. Outside, she spotted Blake with his back to the river, stiff hands gripping the rail alongside his body. Tessa ducked behind the crowd, afraid he had seen her. He hadn't, though his entire body looked tense. Tessa waited for the crowds to part, squeezed off a few quick shots, then put her camera down in time to see Michael and Jillian approaching.

He was holding her elbow and coaxing her forward. Something was terribly wrong. Her usual sharp energy seemed to have vanished.

Michael had seen Tessa. He looked over his shoulder to where her camera had been pointing and turned back with a frown. "What are you doing out here?"

"Getting a picture of Blake. It might help me recognize him." She touched Jillian's arm. "I heard you were sick. Are you feeling better?"

Lackluster eyes met Tessa's. "I feel all right. That's not the problem."

"Inside," Michael said. "In you go, Jillian."

And without waiting to see what Tessa would do, he nudged Jillian forward. Rather than risk another shot of Blake, hoping she had a clear one, Tessa followed her inside.

From Jillian's tripping gait, Tessa wondered how much she'd already had to drink. Unfortunately, when the waitress brought her a kamikazi, Jillian gulped it down immediately and called for another one.

Michael pressed his lips together. Violet, as well, seemed worried.

Gus continued his valiant effort to keep the conversation going. "Where's Blake, anyway?"

"Here." He slipped back into his seat.

"So, friend Blake," Gus said, "three million dollars. Tell us the secret of your success."

"No secret. Good education, good bank. Look at who all I work with."

He was all graciousness now that Michael had arrived, Tessa noticed. She wondered about the exact hierarchy at Chadsworth. Was Michael in charge of their office, so that Blake included him among the people to please?

"Where did you go to school anyway?" Violet was asking.

Whatever Blake had been drinking went down wrong. He sputtered before answering. "Vanderbilt in Tennessee."

Tessa leaned forward. "And where did you work before coming to Singapore?"

"What is this? The third degree?" His hand reached out and crushed his napkin. "If you must know, I worked at banks in Memphis and Little Rock. Would you like to see my résumé?"

"I know someone who went to Vanderbilt, in the Business School even," Tessa said. "And she's about your age."

"I'm not likely to have known her," Blake said. "I didn't have time for socializing."

"And yet you look very familiar to me," Tessa said. "I'm sure we've met before."

His eyes swept over her, as if deigning to see her for the first time. "Not likely again. I'd have remembered you." He made it sound less than complimentary.

But he did remember her. Sincere accent notwithstanding, she knew somehow it must be true. He did, and there was some reason, some dreadful reason, that he didn't want her to remember as well.

He didn't give her a chance to look at him longer. He excused himself and headed toward the rest room. Talk around the table continued without him.

Tessa hugged her arms across her chest. If only she could shake off this feeling of impending danger, she'd be more than happy to let Blake avoid her as much as he wanted. Was the danger for Michael?

She glanced in his direction. He seemed to have missed the entire exchange with Blake. He was whispering something to Jillian instead.

Jillian shook off whatever he was saying and motioned for another drink. Coaxed by Gus, Michael began adding his own lighthearted stories about college to the discussion around the table. A smaller group of bankers from a nearby table soon crowded in among them, and the party became quite boisterous, the topic shifting to banking stories worldwide.

The fun never touched Jillian. Through it all, Tessa could see her brooding, first morose and then militant. Halfway through her fourth drink, she pushed her chair back and rose to her feet. The heavy tumbler smashed onto the table, sloshing liquid over its rim.

"Jillian?" Michael said.

She curled her lip. "You guys don't have the slightest idea."

Michael slipped his hand in hers. "Sit down, Jillian."

"You're as clueless as the rest of them, Michael." She looked around the table, then stumbled back, unsettling her chair.

Michael took the glass from her hand. "We're taking off," he said. For a moment his gaze settled on Tessa, and then he pulled Jillian close against his side. "Come on, Jillian."

The people from the neighboring tables had drifted away. No one at the Chadsworth group said anything until Blake let out a disgusted sound. "I told y'all how she'd be."

Tessa ignored Gus's response and hurried after Michael and Jillian. She caught up with them outside. "Michael?"

He paused.

"Michael! You are coming, aren't you?" Jillian said beside him.

"I'll just be a minute."

Tessa held up her hands. "Please, don't let me stop you. I'll be fine on my own."

He winced. "Sorry. Again not the way I planned for the evening to end." He glanced at Jillian, but she was looking vacantly through the crowds toward the glittering water. "When's your friend coming?" he said.

"His name's Corin, and I'm not sure."

"Leave a message on my machine, will you? I'll check it later."

"But what about the dinner tomorrow at Ivy Tan's parents' house?"

"I'll call in the morning. Now I have to go."

Tessa stood on the sidewalk a minute or two longer after they'd disappeared into the crowd, so that when Blake emerged from Harry's, she easily intercepted him.

"Tessa." He looked the way a man would who woke to find a cockroach on his chest. "I thought you left with Michael and Jillian."

"No, actually, I've been stranded. How about some dinner?"

"No way. Uh, sorry." He smiled and patted his chest pocket. "I just got a call on my cell phone. I gotta get going."

And he, too, vanished, so quickly she was surprised he didn't knock anyone over in his haste.

Tessa shook her head in amazement. At least now she had his picture.

She went back inside to say good-bye to Gus and Violet, Nigel having left much earlier. They invited her to dinner and then took her to a very crowded karaoke bar in Holland Village. By the time she returned to Jillian's apartment, it was past 11:30.

Corin Bolt sat on Jillian's couch.

TEN

Tessa laughed. "I knew you'd show up like this."

He stood and bowed. "Just trying to live up to my name—a bolt out of the blue. And be quiet, will you? They must go to bed with the sun in Ohio. Your roommate wasn't too happy to have me wake her up."

"Jillian's in bed? When did you get here?"

"A little before eleven."

"Let's go into the kitchen then. I'll get you something to drink."

"A beer?"

Tessa pulled open the refrigerator. "Jillian has some, though you might not like her selection."

"Any cold one will do." He leaned past her and helped himself to a Tiger, a local brew that Jillian had taken a liking to. "Not bad. Now, what'd you find out from your cousin Michael?"

She leaned back against the refrigerator. "You didn't get my message, did you? What if he'd said no? What would you have done then?"

He slanted a seductive look at her across the top of his beer bottle. "What do you think?"

She threw a dish towel at him.

"Whoa, whoa. It's hard to resist teasing you."

She stuck out her tongue at him and picked up the phone. Michael answered on the second ring.

"Corin's here."

"Now?"

"He came in on a flight earlier this evening."

"Okay, then, bring him over. I'll have everything ready."

~ ~ ~ ~ ~

Corin Bolt.

Michael had already looked up the man's homepage on the Internet: an adventure photographer with dozens of awards on his mantel, along with two acclaimed photography books. Constantly employed, a world traveller. So popular with photographer wanna-bes that his upcoming workshops were already filled up.

And close enough to Tessa to stop by and see her.

Michael scowled. So what would it be? Fire ants in his bed? A mild poison in his coffee?

He had already warned Mrs. Ling to prepare the second bedroom for a guest and to pick up extra breakfast supplies. He himself was the only thing still unprepared in the apartment, and no amount of time was going to solve that problem.

How could he have been arrogant enough to think there would be no other men in her life?

The doorbell rang. Michael bared his teeth at the sound. *Come in, come in, said the spider to the fly.*

She was laughing up into the man's face when Michael opened the door.

"Michael. This is Corin Bolt. Sorry about the timing."

Tall, well over six feet, athletic body. Older than Michael had expected, closer to forty than thirty. *And wouldn't you know it, a full head of hair.* All that and a smile that would charm a loan off a bankruptcy judge. Michael felt himself shrinking.

"Can we come in?" Tessa said.

He stepped aside. "Let me show you where to put your gear," he told Corin. "Ever been to Singapore before?"

Corin waited till they were in the bedroom. "Yes, and chasing a woman that time, too. Sure can't get anywhere with that cousin of yours."

Michael managed a smile. "She knows what she wants out of life."

"That she does."

"Would you like something to drink?"

"Thanks. I had a beer at Tessa's, but if you have something to eat, that'd be great."

In the kitchen, Tessa was already raiding the refrigerator. "Chinese from Mrs. Ling, fixings for an omelet, or sandwich meats." She saw Michael's raised eyebrows and grinned. "He's always hungry. Hope you don't mind."

"Help yourself."

"A sandwich, I think," Corin said, rubbing his hands. "Just stand aside, I'll fix them."

And fix the sandwiches he did—ham, turkey, bacon, slices of onion and tomato, cheese, lettuce, all layered into a hard roll, with a healthy dollop of hot Chinese mustard on each.

"I did have supper," Tessa protested.

"I'll finish anything you don't want. Dig in."

Michael delayed a moment before biting into the sandwich. This late at night raw onions would inevitably give him heartburn, and yet he'd rather have that than admit a weakness to this man. He resolutely lifted the handful to his mouth, cynicism going down with the sandwich: Let Corin Bolt scale mountains, trek days into the wilderness, brave hostile natives, and confront cataclysmic volcanos. Michael Lawton would eat raw onions to prove his manhood.

"How long have you two known each other?" he asked.

"Since that workshop in northern Virginia, do you remember?" Tessa said.

"Sure, that's where we met, but it wasn't until Lhasa that we got to know each other." Corin swept a napkin over his bulging mouthful. "You were on assignment for *Travel* magazine, on your way to the headwaters of the Mekong River, and I was photographing a trek around Mount Kailas."

"The Buddhist center of the universe," Tessa explained.

"And the Hindu one as well," Corin said. "I was quite taken with Tessa, even back then, and since both assignments meant a trip into Tibet, I convinced her to come with me to circle the mountain. If you don't know, circling anything is a form of prayer for Buddhists, so circling the center of the universe is like the ultimate prayer. It's thirty-two miles around."

"There's a system of interlocking valleys," Tessa said.

Thirty-two miles. No wonder they had bonded.

"We started early in the morning before the sun was up," Corin said, "trekked all day, and ended up under moonlight. And you know what? There really was some kind of spiritual aura to the place. I was amazed at the pictures I got."

Tessa was shaking her head. Was that chagrin Michael saw?

Corin grinned. "Tessa, of course, wouldn't buy it. I think she spent most of the day praying, though not to the Buddha, you can be sure of that, and quoting Scripture to herself as some kind of mantra against evil spirits."

"No," Tessa said. "It wasn't anything like that. I remember wondering that day about natural theology and how close people could come to God on their own, if people could ever know Christ without knowing his name. I did spend a lot of the day in prayer, but it was a plea to God to save the people there, to let their devotion count for something."

"Why don't you just give in and admit that it does?" Corin said. "You've seen enough of the world to know Christians don't have any kind of monopoly on truth."

Tessa winced. "Let's talk about something else, please. Tell us about Mount Erebus and about this assignment in Indonesia."

They talked late into the night. Corin's energy seemed inexhaustible, and he told a very good story. In different circumstances Michael thought he might have been a mercenary, have gun will travel. Instead, he avowed pacifism and deplored big game hunting in particular. A man of obvious passion, he cared deeply about the environment and the plight of oppressed people anywhere and, from what he said, campaigned with equal fervor against the exploitation of the Antarctic and the annexation of Tibet.

The more Michael saw of Corin with Tessa, the smaller Michael felt. She obviously liked and admired him. Was love that much more?

Worse, how many other men like Corin did she have in her life?

When she finally stood to go home, Michael offered to take her, somewhat more forcefully than intended. Corin shrugged and let them go. Perhaps jet lag had finally caught up with him.

"Quite a man," Michael said as they walked down the shadowed sidewalk.

Tessa shrugged. "He's been a good friend. How's Jillian?"

"Was she asleep when you got home?"

"Yes."

Michael was relieved. After leaving Harry's with Jillian, he had purchased coffee and taken her to the Botanic Gardens to walk beside the lake. When she calmed down, they had gone to a nearby McDonald's for a chicken sandwich—anything to dilute the poison in the alcohol she had drunk. Before taking her home, he had wrung a promise from her to go with him to see a counselor affiliated with a campus ministry. He had never seen her so morose.

But then who could blame her?

"She's flying to Hong Kong tomorrow," he said. "Did you know that?"

"When did that come up?"

"Yesterday. It was a last-minute decision. She'll be back late tomorrow evening."

"That reminds me," Tessa said. "About tomorrow night…"

"Yes?"

"Ivy suggested coming by around six."

"I'll pick you up at five-thirty," he said. "Does Corin know about this?"

"It's all set."

"I just have to leave in time to pick up Jillian at the airport." They had come to Jillian's doorway. He almost took her hand, almost touched her arm, yet even as he hesitated, she was backing away. He sighed. "Until tomorrow then. Good night, Tessa."

She woke the next morning at 9:00 to a quiet apartment. It took her a moment to remember Jillian was gone. She burrowed back into her pillow and took a deep, slow breath.

A one-day trip to Hong Kong, and on a Saturday. What business would require that kind of trip?

And yet it must be business—right?—and urgent, if Michael was picking Jillian up at the airport. He must want to talk with her about her trip immediately. Otherwise he'd simply call or wait until she made it back to her apartment on her own.

The phone rang, and Tessa dragged herself up from the bed.

"Hey, it's Corin. Mike says there's windsurfing over near the airport. How about it?"

"Michael's coming?"

"Nope. An early trip to the airport, he said, something about a friend needing a send-off, and then a round or two of golf with some clients. I've got you to myself today, Wander Woman." Tessa could hear the trademark grin in his voice. "Make the most of it."

"Give me thirty minutes, and I'll be ready."

For ten Singaporean dollars an hour, Tessa and Corin rented Windsurfers at the East Coast Sailing Centre and spent most of the day off Changi Point. In the distance freighters plied the channels toward Singapore's busy container ports. As a result, the beach wasn't as clean as Tessa would have liked, but closer in, brilliantly colored sails skimmed across the waters and at least the weather seemed mercifully to be holding off.

Corin spent the first hour teaching Tessa and the next hour coaxing her to try again. Instead, after a quick lunch, purchased from the food stalls directly behind the beach, Tessa rented a large umbrella, pulled out her books on Australia, and let the more avid athlete wear himself out.

At three she flagged him down. He was grinning, the picture of robust health.

"You could keep this up until sundown, couldn't you?" she said.

"I can't believe you quit so quickly. You were just getting the hang of it."

She rubbed her upper arms. "My muscles think I should have quit sooner. Anyway, I'm ready to head back. Stick around here if you want. I know it'll take you less time to get ready."

"Okay. See you later." And he started paddling back out.

She watched him, wondering how late he'd end up making them. Corin had plenty of discipline on assignments. In his personal life, schedule was a dirty word.

The apartment seemed eerily quiet without Jillian. Tessa stood just inside the door for a minute, wondering why she felt so anxious and realized that much of her worry focused on Jillian. How had she managed to engage so much of Michael's attention? What was going on between them?

If it was something at the bank, did it involve Blake, her other source of concern? Time was slipping away fast, with the assignment approaching. If she was going to discover who he was, she needed to do so quickly, yet what more could she do?

Tessa shook her head. All these questions could wait. Her aching muscles couldn't.

Two aspirin and forty-five minutes in the hottest water she could manage, and her upper arms and shoulders felt almost normal. Now for the exterior trappings. For special occasions in hot climates, she carried a sheer lilac print dress with a high neckline and cap sleeves. Fully lined with gossamer fabric, the dress gave Tessa an air of sophisticated elegance. Hanging it in the bathroom steam removed most of the wrinkles that remained from packing; a quick press removed the rest. She added some body to her hair with the curling iron, put on some subtle makeup, and was ready.

They came for her a little before six, not too late, and stood side by side outside her door. Corin wore loose-fitting slacks with a matching vest, unbuttoned, and Michael his more traditional suit and tie.

Tessa grinned at the tie. "I thought you got free from those things during the weekends, Michael."

"Not when I'm having drinks at Tan Lee Ying's house."

"And he thinks *we* never quit working," she told Corin.

He gallantly kissed her hand. "Who's going to notice us

poorly plumed male birds when you're nearby? You look beautiful."

She smoothed her dress down. "You've seen this before, Corin."

"It's not the dress I'm talking about."

Tessa laughed. She gathered up her purse, thrust one arm in Corin's and one in Michael's, and said, "Let's go." Michael, not as charmed as Tessa by Corin's gallantry, felt stiffer than the Tin Man.

"You know Ivy's excited to meet you," she told him in the elevator.

"I figured I'd be her date, yes."

"*Banker* and *unattached* figured prominently in her choice—sorry, Corin."

Michael smiled, though in his eyes, Tessa saw a hint of resignation.

"I won't let you down," he said.

She squeezed his arm. "Thanks for coming."

Corin had stepped forward and was holding the door of the elevator open. "You guys ready? We're going to be late if we don't hurry."

Tessa laughed again. "Like you should complain," she scolded him.

The Tans' house occupied part of a cul-de-sac northwest of the downtown area. From the street, they couldn't see much of the house. A high concrete wall separated it from the road and the other houses crowded around. But they saw plenty of limousines and sports cars parked along the street, and a valet waited to open their taxi door.

Behind the wall, the house seemed much too close to the

front of the lot, but once inside, Tessa could see the reason. Starting near the house and expanding wider as it went, a spacious, shady yard stretched for at least an acre behind the house, with gardens and a swimming pool and even a tennis court.

Solid and almost windowless at the front, the house had a proliferation of glass at the back, its northern exposure bringing in light without the sun's heat. Ivy hadn't been kidding about her parents acquiring a little class. Furnishings were severely modern, quality everywhere, but chiefly, the rooms highlighted that most costly of Singaporean luxuries—space, and lots of it.

Ivy came toward them and cast an impressed gaze upon both Michael and Corin as Tessa introduced them.

"Please, all of you, come and meet my parents, though I understand," she said, shaking a finger at Michael, "that you have already met my father. You must be quite successful for him to remember you so readily."

Michael bowed his head. "Your father is too polite to forget anyone's name, even a lowly name like my own."

Ivy laughed. "Perfectly done. False Asian humility at its best and you even worked in a compliment to my father." She slipped a hand through Michael's arm and smiled up at him. It was a clear violation of Singaporean etiquette for a woman to touch a man, but Ivy's family and friends must expect it of her by now. "Come along," she said to all of them.

Ivy's father smiled and welcomed them, a hint of Ivy's unconventional attitude evident in his laughing eyes. Her mother, more formal, seemed just as pleased to meet them, and even more so when Tessa gave her a framed copy of the photograph she had taken on Ivy's balcony. "And you, too, Mr. Bolt? You also are a photographer?"

"An adventure photographer," Ivy said. "He seems to like anything dangerous—a consummate athlete."

"Ah, then, perhaps you would like to play some golf with me?" Mr. Tan said.

Tessa hid her smile. Corin hated golf. A sport for wimps, he said. Not nearly enough excitement or danger.

"Sorry," he responded to Mr. Tan. "I'll only be here a couple of days."

"Tomorrow morning? I'm sure I can get in at Singapore Island."

"Even so…" Corin bounced his head sideways toward Tessa and shrugged. "We'll be busy, I'm afraid."

"And you, Michael?" Mr. Tan said.

"I'd love to. I've picked up the Singaporean passion during the past three years. But not tomorrow, I'm afraid. Perhaps another time?"

"I'll have my secretary call you," Mr. Tan said.

Ivy took them on a tour of the house, bigger than it appeared from the outside, and then in the garden wandered off with Michael. Tessa avoided looking for them, telling herself to enjoy Corin's company—*making* herself enjoy it. She even managed to look somewhat surprised when Ivy and Michael appeared beside them, asking if they were ready to leave.

"Yes, of course," she said brightly and looked up at Corin. "If you're ready?"

He promptly took her hand—something he knew she didn't normally like—grinned wolfishly down at her, and waved a lavish hand toward the door. "Lead on."

They rode in Ivy's Mustang convertible. Michael, comfortable in the front seat with Ivy, loosened his tie and took off his suit coat, while Corin took advantage of the squashed quarters with Tessa in the back. Torn between wisdom and inclination,

Tessa had no room to maneuver away from Corin's arm. Michael didn't seem interested anyway. He smiled when Ivy held her silk wrap up to catch the wind, responded ironically to Corin's jabs about golf, and generally ignored Tessa entirely.

They ate at the Latour, a restaurant in the Shangri-La Hotel that featured French-based nouvelle cuisine. Overlooking a spectacular view of the gardens, they sat in comfortable rattan chairs, surrounded by urbane diners enjoying elegant crystal, china, and silver place settings. To Tessa, Michael seemed to be at his congenial best, with Corin and Ivy both mellowed by the Latour's excellent wines. She alone felt tense and uncomfortable.

If Michael hadn't been there, she might have had a glass of wine herself, just to help her relax, but since he made a point of abstinence, his reaction might make her more tense than ever.

Of course, if Michael hadn't been there, she wouldn't have needed the glass of wine.

As the leisurely meal ended, Ivy said, "I've reserved two trishaws for an evening tour, if you're interested. You've done this already, I'm sure, Michael, but it's always romantic and the best way to see the downtown area at night. What do you say? Should I call and cancel?"

"Not at all," Corin said. "I'm game. How about you, Tessa?"

"Of course." Though she knew very well how they'd end up being paired.

They took a taxi to the Waterloo Street car park, where they started their trishaw ride under hundreds of lightbulbs, and went from there through Middle Road toward Little India, zigzagging down narrow alleys packed with people and sounds and glowing lights.

"What's the matter?" Corin said along one of these narrow streets. "You don't seem to be enjoying this very much."

"Tired muscles, I suppose." She swept a hand across her upper chest. "Probably the windsurfing."

"Really?" He seemed about to say more, then changed his mind. He chuckled instead and put his arm around her shoulders. "If you're sure that's all it is, relax will you? Staying tight won't help those muscles any."

She nodded and glanced back at the trishaw behind them. Michael was smiling down at an animated Ivy, laughing now at something she said.

"He's fine, you know," Corin said. "She's making a play, but I don't think he's buying."

"Yeah, well, he wouldn't." Tessa crossed her arms and scrunched lower in the seat.

The ride took them further through Old Singapore until they stopped on Albert Street at the Rochore Centre.

"It's not even eleven yet," Ivy said. "How about disco at the Fire? Or jazz at the Saxophone? If you're feeling wild, we could always do a little karaoke at the Java Jive? Or we could play tourist and sip a Singapore Sling at Raffles."

Tessa shook her head. Enough was enough. "Corin kept us up late last night and then had me out windsurfing most of the day. I'm ready to crash."

"It's been a wonderful evening, though," Michael said.

"Corin?"

He glanced at Tessa. "Tempting, but I suppose I should play old man, too." He leaned forward, kissed Ivy on the cheek, and then took Tessa's hand. "Shall we head back in a taxi?"

"Let me call for one," Michael said, already taking out his cell phone. "But I'll see Ivy to her car at the Shangri-La, if you don't mind, and then head on out to the airport. Take my key again, Corin."

"No." Corin waved the key off. "I'll wait at Tessa's apartment."

"It's an extra key," Michael said. "Take it. I'll be late."

Corin shrugged. "Okay."

In the taxi, Tessa leaned her head back against the seat and closed her eyes. When it stopped outside her apartment building, she turned to Corin. "I'm beat. How about going on to Michael's?"

"You kidding? Of course I'm coming up. I resisted pursuing this in the trishaw, but now I want some real answers."

"About what?"

"Come on, girl. Out you go."

ELEVEN

N ow," Corin said, once he had helped himself to a beer and found a Coke for Tessa. "Tell me about this 'cousin' of yours. He's not really your cousin, is he?"

"Why are you asking?"

"Because in a hundred ways tonight you showed more than cousinly feelings toward him."

Tessa's eyes lifted to his, and he laughed.

"Every two minutes," he said, "you were checking his reaction—every time I touched you, after every joke, after every comment from Ivy. And I've never seen you so tense. You've never reacted that way with me. Come on now, fill me in." When she said nothing, he took her hand and squeezed it. "Come on, friend. Your cousin?"

She wrinkled her nose. "My step-cousin. My mother married his uncle. We met about ten years ago for the first time."

"And...? What else?"

"And four years ago I fell in love with him."

"Aaah. And you're still crazy about him."

"No!" Her shoulders slumped. "Yes." She groaned. "Maybe I am. How should I know? I came to Singapore to prove to myself that it was all behind me, and now—" She groaned and bounced her head once or twice on the table. "I don't *want* to feel this way about him. I don't!"

"No kidding...Michael Lawton?"

"I had my chance. He asked me to marry him four years ago, but I couldn't do it. I couldn't turn my back on photography. Even now, if the offer were still open, why would I want to? You know how I feel."

"More than you know," Corin said. "And you're sure that's what Michael wanted—no more photography?"

"Oh, come on, Corin. You know the score. How many marriages survive this lifestyle? One in ten? He wasn't leaving that option open."

She stood up and emptied the dregs of her soda into the sink. When she turned around again, Corin gave her a lazy half-grin.

"What?" she said.

"I suppose this means I should finally stop trying."

"Oh, please." She made a face. "Since we're being so honest with each other, you never were in love with me, and you know it. You'd have taken a quick fling if I'd been willing, but when I finally got it into your thick skull that I wasn't interested, you were just as happy to have someone to talk to who wasn't constantly expecting you to jump into bed with her—and that's been good for both of us." She planted her hands on the table and leaned toward him. "Here's my question for you, Mr. Advice-to-the-Lovelorn. Why is it you've made such a song and dance of pursuing me when we both knew it would never happen? When was the last time you did get involved with someone?"

"What's your point?"

"Maybe you like using me as an excuse not to fall into bed with every woman you meet."

"And why would that be?"

She stuck her hand out, palm up, and made a beckoning motion. "Give me your wallet."

"What?"

"Hey, buddy. I'm playing a hunch here. I've never seen what you keep in there, but I'll bet you anything there's a picture of your ex-wife."

"Anything? Even a night of wild, passionate love?"

"Give it a break. There is, isn't there?"

"What if there is?"

"Come on, Bolt; I want to see the picture of the woman who's kept you pining all these years."

He thrust his fingers through his hair, gave a loud sigh, and reached into his back pocket. "But I *have* been with other women since we split. Don't get any ideas about that."

"Not very satisfying?"

He grunted. "Though if you'd been willing…"

"Give it here," Tessa said.

The woman in the picture was blond like Tessa, but older, closer to Corin's age, with a sweet smile and commonplace features. She was looking down at a child, probably one of Corin's three daughters. With typical brilliance, he had captured the tenderness in the bend of her neck, the passionate warmth in her smile, the unmistakable love in her eyes.

But none of it for Corin. No wonder he looked so glum.

"What's her name?"

"Abby. Abby Bolt. She kept the name for the kids' sake."

The wallet pocket had other pictures behind this one. Tessa pulled them all out and laid them on the table, a photographic diary of his ex-wife that spanned a number of years.

"How long has it been?"

"Five years next month."

"And this last picture, how recent is it?"

"Last summer. I stop by now and then to see the girls…" He shrugged. "And Abby, sure. As often as I can. I would have gone there this weekend, except the two older girls are on a winter retreat somewhere." He smiled cynically. "No reason to go if the kids aren't there."

"She's never married again?"

"No."

Tessa clasped his hand in both of hers. "Then why don't you go and use that famous charm on her? Win her back!"

Corin rubbed the back of his neck, weariness apparent. "We've known each other since junior high, were sweethearts all through high school and college. I wrote her every day back then, if you can believe it. When I finished, we married even though she had two years left, and then I started getting serious about my work. It wasn't so bad, I suppose, being gone for such long periods of time while she was in school. That kept her busy enough. And then she worked as a newscaster at the local television station for a couple of years, and that wasn't so bad either.

"But then Kelly was born. I was in Zaire for two months for the *National Geographic* and couldn't make it back for her birth. And then Teresa. Missed birthdays, weeks and months apart. It was hard, you know, coming back from location, full of experiences and excitement, with her wanting to talk about whether Teresa's preschool was too academic and how to convince Kelly to keep her room clean, and what happened to the plumber's check I had promised to send."

He sighed. "By the time Abby got pregnant with Michelle we were already in trouble. Michael's right, Tessa. This life's murder on a marriage. Now, since we split, she's been starring in a cooking show, believe it or not. She's got her own life. The kids are older. She wouldn't be counting on me so much, I think. *Now* we could probably make it. But I'm not about to ask her. Too easy for her to say no." He shook his head. "I couldn't take it."

Tessa grimaced. If she'd wanted proof…"Do you spend much time with her when you see the girls?"

"Hardly at all. She clears out and leaves us alone. I tell you,

Tessa, I don't have a snowball's hope in hell."

"No one has hope in hell, don't you know that? But heaven…" She smiled. "Heaven has hope to spare—and might have plans for you even yet."

"Oh, brother. Keep you up late enough, Wander Woman, and this is where it takes you. Must mean it's time for me to take off."

Tessa laughed. At the front door of the apartment, she said, "What about tomorrow?"

"You're going to church, right? Come eat breakfast with me. My plane leaves at ten-fifteen."

"Eight okay?"

"Make it seven-forty-five. I'll come by." He gave her a quick kiss on the cheek. "You're a good friend, Tessa. I'm *almost* glad we never slept together."

She gave him a shove and watched as he walked toward the elevator. He blew her a kiss as the doors closed.

Michael was waiting at the door of the church the next morn-ing. "Do you want to go back to the same Sunday school?"

"With you? Of course."

"Then follow me."

And those were pretty much the only words he said to her until they parted after Sunday school. "You're on your way to children's church, aren't you?" he said then. When she nodded, he added, "Good. Because I have some people to talk to before church. Meet me afterward where you came in this morning."

She almost saluted as he walked away.

Did he think last night had been fun for her? And what had he been doing out so late with Jillian anyway? Perhaps Michael's surliness today came from lack of sleep.

She stood in the hall where he'd left her, staring after him, people slipping by her, giving her curious glances, children bumping her accidentally. She finally noticed, shook her head at the man who asked if she needed some help, and turned to make her way to the room where children's church met. Though the children didn't come until just before the sermon, she would need some time to set up.

...As well as time to pack up.

She took so long Michael came to look for her.

"Almost done," she told him, putting the last of the model releases in her pack. "Just one more detail, Martha. Could you tell me where else you've led children's church?"

Michael continued to wait by the door, his face revealing nothing of his feelings.

Then how did she know so well he was getting impatient, especially when the feeling was so rare for him?

"You should have gone ahead on your own," Tessa said when they were in the taxi. "I could have made my way back to Jillian's apartment."

"No. It's just that I managed to convince Jillian to eat lunch with us, and I'm afraid she'll change her mind. You don't have plans, do you?"

Tessa shook her head. "She's not feeling sick again?"

"No, not *feeling* sick. In fact..." He paused, changed his mind, and didn't say anything more.

She pulled out her note pad and made a show of checking through her captions. Nothing left to do there except enter them in her laptop, but if he didn't want to talk, fine. She wasn't going to let him think it bothered her.

"I have this taxi for a half-day rental," he said at the apartment building. "You wait here while I go up and get Jillian."

"She might still be in bed," Tessa objected.

He shook his head. "I have a better chance of convincing her to come on my own."

More confused than ever, Tessa let Michael get away without her photo equipment. She had intended leaving it at the apartment, but after Michael's stern instructions, she wasn't about to follow him up.

It took twenty minutes for them to return, leaving Tessa plenty of time to imagine how Michael managed to extract Jillian from her bed and convince her to get dressed. She came down wearing denim shorts and a plain green shirt. Even more uncharacteristically, she had pulled her hair into a simple ponytail and wore no makeup that Tessa could see. She really did look sick.

Tessa scooted to the far side so that Jillian could sit in the middle.

"So, where shall I tell him?" Michael said. "Someplace in particular?"

"Anyplace that I won't see someone I know," Jillian said.

"You had a big breakfast, didn't you?" Michael asked Tessa. When she said yes, he directed the taxi to the Choon Seng Restaurant on Ponggol Road. "It'll be a thirty- or forty-minute drive," he told Tessa, "but it's well away from the city and serves excellent seafood. And then afterwards we can walk along the beach."

Obviously this was all for Jillian's sake. Tessa began having the most insane urge to cross her arms and stick her lower lip out. Before she knew it she'd be stomping her foot as well.

She swallowed the impulse and smiled at Jillian. "Feeling any better?"

"Not much," Jillian muttered, "but Michael's insisting I get out." The rearview mirror proved irresistible. "I'm a mess. I can't believe I'm doing this. Take me back, please, Michael."

"Do you have some makeup Jillian can use?" Michael said.

"No!" Jillian threw up her hands. "What are you thinking, Michael? I can't use someone else's makeup." She crossed her arms and sank back lower against the seat. "I can't believe this is happening."

Michael took her hand and held it firmly in his. "Some sunshine, a decent meal—you're going to feel better, Jillian."

She made a move to pull her hand away, but Michael hung on, determined.

"You'll see," he told her. "Everything's going to be fine."

On the other side of Jillian, Tessa drew back further into her own corner. She was beginning to feel a little extraneous, to put it mildly. No wonder Carol de Vos had asked about Jillian. Tessa and Michael had been almost engaged, had even skirted the issue of marriage, before he had held her hand like that. His standards had slipped during the past four years.

They left the city traffic behind, passing pig farms and fish ponds and finally, as they neared the ocean, mangrove swamps. During the trip, since Jillian didn't seem interested in talking, Tessa asked Michael about seafood on the island, and how often he ate at this distant restaurant, and if he'd ever tried windsurfing. Michael did his part, but it was hard going.

The taxi took them to a half-concrete, half-wooden building close to the water, with some kind of metal roof. Happy the cramped taxi ride was over, Tessa followed Michael and Jillian to a table outside. Jillian's jeans and T-shirt blended well with the casual atmosphere of the Choon Seng. Michael had obviously chosen with her in mind. Looking around, Tessa found it hard to believe such country surroundings existed so close to downtown Singapore.

"Chili crab," Michael said as soon as they sat down.

Jillian winced. "I don't know, Michael."

"Come on." He grinned across the table at her. "You'll enjoy the sensation of smashing the shells anyway."

A hint of her customary humor flitted across Jillian's face. "Yeah. Maybe."

"They're almost a national dish," Michael explained to Tessa. "They stir-fry the crabs in garlic and soy sauce—"

"And lots of chili," Jillian inserted.

"And then pile them in a bunch in the middle of the table, give us a hammer each, and let us go at them. Plenty messy, but almost as much fun as flavor."

Tessa smiled. "I'm game."

"We'll throw in some fried *sotong*—"

"Squid," Jillian said.

"And some spinach in prawn sauce and, of course, some of the Cheng Soon's famous fried noodles."

Squid…and Tessa had accused Michael of shunning Nonya food, certainly more conventional than this.

"Sounds fine," she said. "A real adventure."

As the meal progressed, as messy as Michael promised, Tessa decided his therapy was working. Jillian laughed at Tessa's first taste of crab—a sharp shock of red pepper sauce followed by a more mellow aftertaste of flavor. She teased Michael when he refused to order a beer with her, smiled when the waiter hollered out her order for more noodles, and generally looked much more relaxed at the end of the meal than when she started.

"What now?" Michael said. He had his chin propped up on one hand and was smiling across the table at them. "Shall we head down to Sentosa and show Tessa how Singaporeans have fun? Or maybe the Haw Par Amusement Park. We keep talking about going."

Somehow, as Michael spoke, Jillian's pleasure collapsed, like a fast leak in a helium balloon. "No," she said. "I don't want to."

Regret flickered in Michael's eyes. "Then a walk along the beach?"

She didn't respond.

"Jillian?"

"You know what I'd like?" She was staring down at the shattered remains of her meal. "I want to get on a boat, a fast one, to go and go and go as far out from this island as I can, so that just for a little while I can convince myself I can get away from all this." She lifted her eyes to Michael's. "Can we do that? Please? Will you take me?"

"Of course." He held Jillian's gaze for a long moment, then nodded and turned toward Tessa. "You'll come, won't you? It looks like a sunny afternoon, and it's always cooler on the water."

"I don't think so." She resisted the urge to look from Michael to Jillian. "I have some work from this morning that I should finish up, putting notes onto the computer and so forth."

"It won't keep?"

"No."

She took out her purse to pay her share of the meal, but Michael shook his head. "I'll take care of it. And take the taxi. We'll find another way home."

"Okay, if you're sure. Jillian, I'll see you later?"

Jillian nodded.

Tessa left the restaurant as confused as ever. Jillian had made no secret of her attraction to Michael, and yet for a woman who'd be spending a long afternoon alone with him, she didn't seem too excited.

Tessa shook her head and sighed.

In a few weeks, she'd be leaving Singapore anyway. What business was it of hers?

~~~~~

She spent the rest of the afternoon doing laundry and catching up on correspondence. For supper, around seven, she took a big bowl of vanilla ice cream smothered with extra-dark chocolate sauce out onto the balcony. It melted fast. She would have been better off in the air-conditioned apartment, but she felt trapped inside, very much on edge, waiting for Michael and Jillian to return. Her curiosity kept her at the apartment, but she preferred that they find her outside—a feeble attempt at distance.

As it was, she was inside again when they came back around nine. She had set up her small light box to view transparencies and was sitting on the couch, choosing the best ones and revising captions as necessary.

Jillian took two steps into the apartment. "You're here." She looked Tessa over and shrugged. "I'm ready for bed anyway. Thank you, Michael. I think I'll be fine now…better anyway."

She paused near the doorway, waiting for Michael to say good night.

"I'll stick around a while," he said, "and talk to Tessa, if you don't mind?"

"Of course not. Come on in. I suppose you want something to eat."

"Tessa can help me out if I get hungry. Don't worry about me."

Jillian frowned, glanced from Michael to Tessa, then shrugged. "Okay then." And she turned toward her bedroom.

Michael dropped down into the seat opposite Tessa and blew out a long breath. He was obviously tired. Why didn't he go off to bed as well? Instead, he just sat and watched as she lifted a sheet off the light box, replaced it with a new one, and searched through it for shots she could use, and then did it all again.

He finally roused himself. "What are you doing?"

Much as she had with Hugo, she explained the process of eliminating bad shots. "For most stories, I try to fill one slide tray—that's eighty slots—with good photos. That gives the picture editor at the magazine enough to work with."

"From those, how many will the editor choose?"

She frowned. "You look awfully tired, Michael. Why don't you go home, go to bed?"

"No, I'm curious. Let me see." He came to sit beside her on the couch and leaned toward the light box.

He was very close. She could see the stitching on the collar of his shirt, could even smell the faint remnant of his aftershave. A surprisingly dark stubble was beginning to shadow his jaw, and from this angle she couldn't miss the line of muscles running from his shoulders, down his arm, and into his hands. His hands... Her breath caught. She knew those hands.

She jumped up and stumbled around the coffee table to the open floor beyond. "How about some ice cream? I found some incredible English chocolate sauce at a deli nearby, and there are some pecans in the freezer that I'm sure Jillian wouldn't mind sharing."

She pushed through the swinging door into the kitchen without waiting for his response. Forget friend, forget acquaintance—she had to get out of Singapore before she made a complete idiot of herself.

She banged two bowls onto the table and was reaching for the ice cream by the time he joined her.

Jillian followed him in. "Hey, I want some," she said. Her wet hair hung loose to her shoulders, and she now wore cotton pajamas and a plaid housecoat.

Tessa blinked. If Jillian was hoping to attract Michael, she was being pretty crafty in her choice of nightwear.

"Well?" Jillian said. "Is there enough for all of us?"

Tessa grabbed another bowl. "You dish it out, Jillian. I'll warm up this fudge sauce. Since you're here, can we use the pecans from the freezer?"

Once served, Tessa looked with dismay at the pile in her bowl. She had intended only a small helping, just enough to keep Michael company, but Jillian had filled the bowl to over-flowing.

Oh, well, perhaps the chocolate sauce would help calm her down.

Michael looked more tired than ever, but Jillian seemed to have gotten her second wind. Tessa gritted her teeth and fought back an impulse to empty her bowl over Jillian's head. She'd had him all day, after all…

She smothered the thought with a mouthful of straight chocolate sweetness.

"How was the water?" she asked Jillian.

"Fine. We stayed out until after five. Poor Michael. And then he was sweet enough to take me for a walk along the beach." She grinned slyly and, though she addressed her words to Tessa, she kept watching Michael. "And when we got to a nice, quiet, secluded spot, I finally gave in and let Michael do something he's been longing to do since we first met."

"Jillian!"

She waved her hand at Michael. "Stop fretting. It's not what most men want, Tessa. If you must know, I finally let Michael give me his spiel about God."

"Oh."

"Exactly. Oh." Jillian rolled her eyes. "It seems, from what Michael says, that I can strike a deal with this God of yours, just believe and everything's okay. Of course then I'm stuck having to do what he tells me."

Michael would have spoken, but Jillian held up her hand to him and directed her gaze at Tessa. "Is that true?"

Tessa pressed her lips together. She had no idea what to say, and with Michael sitting there... "Well—"

"A law-giving God, Michael says, but don't you think that's just too Singapore—the paternalistic dictator who provides forgiveness and eternal life and all that good stuff and in return demands that I give up everything I love." Jillian glared down into her ice cream bowl, a melted mess of white cream and brown sauce. "In Singapore, people make deals all the time, sacrifice freedoms, give up their rights—*anything* to stay out of trouble. 'Cause if you mess up, watch out. Who *wants* it?" She pushed her bowl away and stood up. "I'm going to bed. No, don't get up, Michael. I don't need anything."

He followed her anyway. Tessa could hear them talking quietly in the hallway. She was washing the dishes when he returned, and he came to stand with his back against the counter beside her, his slumped shoulders forming a continuous arc into crossed arms. "I talked about God's love, you know. Not just about his laws. She made it sound too one-sided."

"I'm sure you did, Michael."

And your own feelings, too? Did they come up?

"But I did convince her to go to church with us next week," he said.

"That's great."

She had to ask him. She didn't care anymore what happened. She had to know what was going on.

"Michael—"

"Do you know, you've been here a whole week," he said. "More than that even. It's hard to believe."

She blinked uncertainly.

"What will you do this week?"

"I saw your pastor on Friday. He gave me some ideas of Christian activities here to photograph."

He turned, leaned his forearms against the counter, and lifted his face to watch hers. "You talked about doing something similar in Kazakhstan. Are these for a mission magazine, too?"

"No, a private project I'm working on." She laid out the washcloth and let the dishwater drain away.

He touched her arm. "Tell me what you're doing."

"You're tired, Michael. You should go home."

"Ah. You're tired, too." He sighed. "Very well. I'll be going. I'll try to call tomorrow if I can. Good night."

The apartment seemed dull without him. She began to put her transparencies away but after a moment stopped and leaned her head wearily against the back of the sofa instead.

She couldn't deny the truth anymore. Whatever had been there with Michael four years ago still waited, like a plant covered over for winter with life in it yet. She would never feel this way about another man. Never.

She let out a long sigh. *Please—one was enough.*

But something was happening between Michael and Jillian, something special and tender and very caring. Michael would never marry a woman who didn't follow Jesus Christ, Tessa knew that, but he might fall in love with one. And now Jillian was asking questions and had promised to go to church with Michael. Jillian's conversion seemed a very real possibility. And if that happened, Michael would be free to marry her—

Tessa froze. What was she thinking? She let out a long, slow, depressing groan.

This was what she had come to: so jealous of Michael that she would begrudge Jillian's eternal destiny, rather than see him find happiness with her.

I'm so sorry. She lowered her face into her hands and

pressed fingertips against an aching head. *Please, really, I didn't mean it. If that's what you want, I'm okay—I'm happy. Whatever else, please—please—help Jillian find out who you really are....*

And let me get out of here before I do something even more stupid.

She put away her supplies with a heavy heart. The two bowls of ice cream didn't help.

TWELVE

In the morning, still troubled about Jillian, Tessa sat down at the kitchen table to plan her day. A return trip to Serangoon Street would get her mind back on work. But no, she had overslept and missed the best light, and somehow she couldn't face the idea of more strangers anyway. She would use the morning to think about Blake instead. Detective Tessa back on the case. It beat sighing over lost love.

She went first to the studio Ivy had recommended to get her transparencies developed, then to a one-hour photo shop to get a print of Blake's picture. That in hand, she headed to the university library, where she painstakingly looked through every travel magazine, every publication, every tourist brochure that she could find that had any of her photographs, just in case something jogged her memory.

The library didn't have everything, but it had enough to keep her busy until two in the afternoon. When she reached the last magazine, she crossed her arms and glared at the picture of Blake propped up against a stack of books. Such common features. Where had she seen him?

He claimed they'd never met, but she didn't believe him. She thought perhaps she had taken his picture somewhere, caught his image without him knowing, and it was her use of that picture that he now resented. But a review of her work wasn't yielding any results. She stared at his picture again and tried to superimpose his image onto another background, some other scene.

Still nothing.

A younger man, thinner? A different color hair? Maybe some acne?

She had no idea, and staring at the picture of him outside Harry's wasn't helping. She only wished she could transfer some of her concern to Michael.

She spent the rest of the afternoon setting up appointments to photograph Christian activities in Singapore. Monday evening, through a contact, she was invited to one of the cell groups of a large and flourishing Singaporean church, which ran all its programs through these small meetings, rather than through the church body as a whole. The group met in one of the downtown housing developments, where a vigorous Chinese woman in her sixties led a rousing discussion. She was a soon-to-retire professor of history, Tessa found out.

Seeing the people pray and worship and study the Word, Tessa was impressed by their commitment to a rational understanding of their faith. Simon had it only half right, she decided: It wasn't just the group that gave faith its validity. It was also the validity that gave faith to the group. She grinned. *So there!*

One of the cell's members, a recent graduate from the university, knew someone in the campus drama troupe and arranged for Tessa to meet her friend the next day. As always, once people knew what Tessa was trying to do, they willingly helped.

Michael's message when she came in a little before ten was brief: he was sorry he had missed her. He had a business engagement the next evening. He'd try calling her if he didn't get in too late.

"You heard the message?" Jillian called from her bedroom.

Tessa heard blues. She pushed Jillian's door open to find the room in shadows, with only one small light breaking the darkness. Jillian was in bed, curled up on one side, her cover pulled high up over her shoulders. The radio on her headboard played softly in the darkness.

"Yes. Thanks." Tessa frowned. "You okay? Hard day?"

"Work, meeting, dinner. Nothing special."

"Want to have lunch tomorrow?"

"No." Jillian's pillow muffled the response. "Too much to do."

"You aren't hungry now, are you?" Tessa said. "I brought home Thai—"

"Ugh, no." She must have seen Tessa's concern. "Don't mind me. Nothing sounds good."

"Jillian, if you would tell me what's happening…"

"No. *No.* Not again." Jillian turned over, her back toward the door. "I'll be fine."

"Sleep well, then. I'll be back late tomorrow night as well."

Tessa had dinner the next evening with some members from the drama troupe, wishing as they talked that she could somehow get on film the struggles they told her about in their ministry. The government in Singapore had made it harder and harder for Christians to speak out about their faith, and yet even as they clamped down, more and more students at the university were turning to Christ.

"If only we could know for sure why," one of the young women confided to Tessa. "Too many, I am afraid, join the church as a career move, an attempt to identify with the wealth of the West. How many really love Jesus?"

They moved later to a coffeehouse, where singers performed contemporary Christian songs in both English and Chinese, with more opportunities for pictures. She stayed out so late that when she got in, Jillian's room was already dark. No message from Michael. Good.

Wednesday evening, Tessa visited the Tamil church and after the service went to the pastor's house for a late supper with his family. She found herself entranced by their love for Jesus. How often would she have to sit with people like the Venugopals before she understood in her heart that Jesus wasn't Western or Eastern or bound by any culture on earth at all?

Getting in late again, though, Tessa began to wonder when people in Singapore slept.

On Thursday evening, she came into the apartment shortly before six to find Jillian on the couch, hanging up the phone.

"Tessa. Michael asked how you were doing. I couldn't say much since I haven't seen you since—when was it—Monday? He's in KL until late tomorrow evening."

Tessa lowered her photo bag to the floor. "KL...oh, Kuala Lumpur. Business, I suppose?"

"As always." Jillian watched with crossed arms as Tessa unbuckled her waist packs and took the chair opposite the couch. "You've been busy."

Tessa heaved a sigh and let her arms hang slack to the floor. "All week. I think I've shot almost a hundred rolls of film and now I've got all the work of organizing them before my assignment starts Saturday morning." She rolled her head around, trying to loosen the muscles in her neck. "You know, I've been calling Blake off and on all week. I've left messages on his machine, with his housekeeper, at the bank. He refuses to contact me. The one time I finally caught him, you'd think I was a telemarketer, he hung up so fast."

"Why would you want him anyway?"

"Well..." Tessa gave a sheepish grin. "The truth is, I'm absolutely sure that I've seen him somewhere before. I can't shake the feeling. I thought if I could eat with him, you know spend a little time looking at him across a table, it might come to me why he looks so familiar."

"Count yourself lucky that you missed him," Jillian said. "I'd rather never go out again than go out with that guy."

When Tessa emerged from a leisurely shower, Jillian was curled up on the couch watching Alfred Hitchcock's *The Man Who Knew Too Much*. A barely eaten pizza sat on the coffee table.

"This looks like fun," Tessa said.

Jillian shrugged. "I tried the blues approach. That just made me feel worse. Now I'm trying the escapist route. It's not working much better. Want some pizza?"

Tessa sighed. She'd appreciate answers even more. But she said, "Sure," and settled down to watch the movie.

Later, still hungry after Jillian had gone to bed, Tessa squeezed some lemon juice over a half-eaten papaya she found in the fridge and sat down at the kitchen table. Jillian was right about one thing. She had enjoyed the evening much more without Blake.

She took his picture from her purse, propped it up against her water glass, and stared at it while she finished the papaya. It was so close, his name. She held herself perfectly still, willing herself to relax.

Nothing.

Maybe she wasn't going back far enough. Maybe it was her college yearbook and pictures she needed. She glanced at her watch: Seven-thirty. If she called now, she'd still catch her father and Jenny before they left for work.

She frowned. She might as well ask for her high school pictures as well.

~ ~ ~ ~ ~

After a morning spent on errands, Tessa returned to the apartment on Friday and finished transferring captions for the pictures she had taken during the previous week to her computer files. When the phone rang around two o'clock, she waited, intending to let the machine take the message.

Then Michael came on the line. She couldn't even remember moving.

"Tessa! I'm glad I caught you. I only have a few minutes before my next meeting."

Was he hoping to reach Jillian? Perhaps he needed to leave a message. She grabbed some paper, ready to take it down.

"Tessa? Are you there?"

"Yes!"

"I'm sorry we've missed each other all week. What have you been doing?"

"Oh." She set the pencil down. "I've been working on my worldwide church project. Wait. I haven't told you about that, have I? I mean, I will…" She tried again. "How's your work in Kuala Lumpur?"

"Fine. Just work. So, your mysterious project involves the worldwide church. That sounds intriguing."

"I'll show you the first chance I get."

"I'm coming home later tonight. You could show me at lunch tomorrow."

"I can't. My assignment starts in the morning."

"Breakfast?"

"I'm sorry. I can't even go to church this week, it's going to be so hectic."

"I see."

"I know—let me give you my cell phone number. I'll be with my family all week, but you could try calling."

There was a pause and the rustle of paper. "All right. Go ahead. I'm ready."

She gave him the number. Sensing that he was ready to hang up, she quickly added that Jillian seemed better. "She's been going to work and eating a little more."

"I'm glad to hear it. Now I have to go. Time for that next meeting. Good-bye, Tessa."

He hung up, the dial tone sounding. Tessa sat staring at the receiver. All week she'd managed to avoid him, then one sound of his voice, and she gave him her cell phone number? She flopped over sideways on the couch and groaned. *Good thinking.*

As always before a major assignment, panic was building. She had staved it off with work during the week, but it arrived in earnest after Michael called. Jillian rang up later in the afternoon and asked if Tessa wanted to meet the group at Harry's, but Tessa said no. She couldn't possibly deal with Blake in this condition.

She kept imagining problems with the assignment. What if the family didn't photograph well? What if they didn't like Tessa and felt inhibited in her presence? What if the weather didn't cooperate or the furnishings in their apartment cluttered every background? And what if Michael was right and the publishers wanted a certain kind of picture, one that would glorify family life rather than reflect reality? She was bound to fail.

When Jillian arrived home a little before midnight, Tessa was on the couch eating Kentucky Fried Chicken and watching an old western on television.

Tessa eyed Jillian suspiciously. Had she met Michael at the airport? Is that why she was so late? Tessa scowled. This was panic talking. She took another bite of drumstick. *Get a grip.*

"I thought you'd go to bed early," Jillian said.

"Couldn't sleep. Too nervous."

"But you're the intrepid photographer," Jillian said, "cool in every situation."

"Now you know. I'll be all right once I get started."

Jillian came around the coffee table, plucked up one of the many sheets spread out beside Tessa, and began reading: "Cooking shots, watching television, school, playground… What is this?"

"That's a shooting list—a feeble attempt to predict the shots I should try to get."

"Why feeble?"

"Because until I get there, how can I know? I need to see their apartment, analyze the lighting, find out how they fill their time." Tessa shuddered. "No, more than that: It's the family that matters, and how can I know how to capture who they are until I actually meet them?"

"Then why make the lists?"

Tessa waved a floppy hand. "Makes a change from chicken."

Jillian laughed. "You're getting giddy." She dug into the box herself. "Shouldn't you go to bed? If you sit up watching John Wayne on the tube, how will you be ready for morning?"

"I'm too tense, I can't sleep. But given the fat content of this chicken—" and Tessa gave another wave of her drumstick, "my system's bound to shut down pretty soon, don't you think?"

"That so?" Jillian stared at the piece in her hand. "Then maybe I should have another one. I could do with a decent night's sleep myself." She must have become aware of Tessa's watchfulness. "Don't start. I'm fine. It's just been a long week." She nodded toward the television. "Which of his movies is this anyway?"

~~ ~~ ~~ ~~ ~~

At a morning meeting the next day, Ivy introduced the ten photographers—one other besides Tessa was American, three were European, one Japanese, and the other four Singaporean—then explained procedures and sent them out. Tessa's family lived in Marine Parade, one of the many housing units administered by the HDB—Housing and Development Board. Charlotte Lim, assigned as Tessa's liaison for the first meeting, went with her in the taxi.

Once there, Tessa climbed out and looked around. On one side of the busy street stood a coffeeshop and hairdressers, a laundry, bookshop, and medical clinic, and numerous food-stalls selling vegetables, fruit, poultry, and fish. Behind these shops and across the street, the HDB apartments towered above them, all white, with lines of windows stretching in orderly fashion up the twenty or more floors of the buildings. Poles with laundry hanging from them stuck out from many of the windows, giving the side of the building a ragged front.

"This way," Charlotte said and led the way to the third floor of one of the HDB units.

Alerted by two boys and a girl who had been waiting for her arrival, two men met Tessa in the corridor. The older, in his forties at the most, stepped forward. "We are so pleased to meet you, Miss Brooks," he said. His hand clasp, though brief, was warm and firm, and his smile looked genuine. "May I introduce myself? I am Soon Heng, this is my brother, Soon Khim, and these are my children, Ah Mooi, Ah Chye, and Ah Kheng."

"How do you do?" With a deferential nod of her head, she added the Chinese equivalent: *"Ni hao ma?"*

"Hao, hao," the two men said, while the children, suddenly shy, hung back.

The second man, Soon Khim, stepped forward as well. Much younger than his brother, perhaps thirty, if that, he had an easygoing smile. "We have been very excited about your arrival, as you can imagine. Days and weeks of anticipation. Thank goodness, you are finally here!"

Soon Heng seemed concerned about Tessa's reaction. "No lah!"

"I've been full of anticipation myself," Tessa reassured him. "I think you're wonderful to allow me to photograph you."

To this Soon Heng nodded and smiled. "No, no. It is nothing. No problem. If you would like to come in, we have prepared a small meal to welcome you."

Instructed to leave her bags in a corner, Tessa took a seat in the living room. Though small, the room had been cleaned almost to the point of scrubbing the paint off the walls. A couch lined one wall, with a matching chair nearby, a coffee table, and a throw rug. Across the room, prominently displayed, a small Buddhist altar held a six-inch laughing Buddha, flanked by two bunches of incense. Beside it, a hutch held family treasures—figurines, vases, a fan, and china—and in the corner sat a television.

Tessa could hear activity in the kitchen, and within moments Soon Heng had led three women out to meet her, all of them pleasantly attractive.

"My mother, Miss Brooks: Soon Ah Lan. And my wife, Mei Ah Koh. And this is my wife's niece, Mui Chin."

A slight woman, Soon Heng's mother was dressed in a brightly colored sarong with an embroidered blouse, her hair wound into a bun at the back of her head. Her face shone with kindness. She took Tessa's hand in hers and said something in a dialect Tessa didn't recognize.

Soon Khim interpreted. "My mother says she is sorry the

165

meal is so simple, that we cannot offer much, and that she wishes she could have made you something special."

Humor again shone in Soon Khim's eyes, and this time Tessa knew why. Without a doubt, a delicious and varied meal awaited Tessa, with more food than she could possibly eat.

"Tell her," Tessa said, "that I'm sure anything made by her hand is very special. I can see how well she has fed her family!"

Soon Khim laughed and translated, earning a further hand clasp for Tessa from his mother.

And indeed, the feast laid out that day rivaled the best food Tessa had eaten in Singapore: chicken and beef dishes and numerous vegetables Tessa couldn't recognize, along with tasty pieces of fish wrapped with chilis in coconut palm leaves, fresh fruit slices, and so much more that Tessa couldn't keep track of it all. The colorful, aromatic dishes lined up along the center of the table so distracted Tessa that she almost forgot why she was there. The family had begun eating before she remembered and excused herself to get her cameras.

"Only a few," she promised, "as a record of this wonderful meal. Please keep eating."

She tried a few different angles. The best came from pushing a stool into the far corner of the living room. She held her arm against the wall as a makeshift tripod and took a wide-angle shot from above. She also set up the real tripod just above table level to get a panoramic close-up of the food. Fortunately the Soon family was easygoing enough to keep talking and laughing among themselves.

Although the grandmother, Soon Ah Lan, spoke mostly dialect—"from the Teochew district in China," Soon Heng explained—everyone else spoke English well enough to converse with Tessa. As the afternoon progressed, she found herself wishing she could forget photographing them and simply visit and get to know them. She did set aside her cameras for the rest of that first meal, which continued in desultory fashion for several hours.

After the meal, Soon Ah Lan excused herself to sit on the couch with some mending, Mui Chin took the three children outside to the playground, and Charlotte departed as well, her work of introduction finished.

That left Tessa at the table with Soon Heng, his wife Mei Ah Koh, and the younger brother, Soon Khim. They sat in a row across from her, expectant, watchful, waiting for her next move.

"That was a wonderful meal and a wonderful introduction to your family."

They nodded their acknowledgment. Soon Khim spoke the obligatory, "It was nothing."

And then they waited again.

"I think what would help me," Tessa said, "is to hear your regular schedule, what the week ahead looks like for each of you. Could we do that?"

Relieved, they all nodded. Tessa pulled her notebook from her backpack, extracted a pencil, and spent the next hour or so taking detailed notes on their family life.

Soon Heng, who worked six days a week at an orchid farm, had taken the day off to greet Tessa. His wife, Mei Ah Koh, who also usually had school on Saturday mornings, had arrived scant minutes before Tessa. The grandmother, Soon Ah Lan, stayed home, cooking and cleaning for the family.

The younger brother, Soon Khim, worked long hours at a television station. The proud holder of a degree in cinematography from a film institute in Hong Kong, he had recently returned to Singapore after three years at a film company there. He was working his way up at the local station now. When things improved, Soon Khim would move into his own apartment—"With a wife?" his mother, Soon Ah Lan, inserted slyly.

"Mothers are always anxious to see children married," Mei Ah Koh explained after translating for Tessa. "When Soon Khim has a wife, Mum can relax."

Mui Chin, the younger, college-age woman, was Mei Ah Koh's niece. She had lived with Mei Ah Koh's family since birth and had come with Mei Ah Koh as a younger sister when she had married Soon Heng seven years earlier. Her presence was an arrangement based both on affection and the availability of a free bed in Soon Ah Lan's room. Mui Chin was now taking a university course, hoping to qualify for medical school.

The three children had both Western and Chinese names. The family called the daughter, aged five, Ah Mooi; and the two boys, aged three and two, Ah Chye and Ah Kheng.

It took a little while, but Tessa eventually picked up the system of names. Under most circumstances people used both the family name and the individual name—Soon Heng or Soon Khim, with a married woman continuing to use her own family name—Mei Koh. But with family members, children, and the elderly, Teochew people often exchanged Ah for the family name or simply inserted the word into the name—Ah Mooi or Soon Ah Lan.

Later, Tessa photographed the evening routine: the niece, Mui Chin, giving Ah Chye and Ah Kheng their bath, Soon Khim helping the little girl Ah Mooi review something for school, the grandmother, Soon Ah Lan, holding Ah Kheng as he fell asleep in front of the television. Tessa couldn't help wondering at the wisdom of highlighting an extended family like Soon Heng's. Perhaps all the well-educated professional women who were rebelling against marriage and children would be more willing if they had the support Mei Ah Koh had at home.

THIRTEEN

I'm not interrupting anything, am I?"

"Michael! No. We're watching television. Let me go out onto the balcony."

Saturday night, when Michael first called the number for Tessa's cell phone, the Soon family couldn't help but notice her reaction. She'd felt doubly awkward speaking in front of them and had withdrawn to the stairwell outside. That hadn't worked for long, since she had quickly attracted a variety of spectators. Back inside, Mei Ah Koh suggested the small balcony off the living room. It worked so well that tonight, when Michael called, Tessa retreated immediately to the hard concrete surface outside.

Somehow talking over the phone proved even easier than talking over food, and she found herself considering the possibility that they could after all part as friends, especially since most of their contact would be long distance—e-mail, telephone, letters—and maybe by the time he married someone else, "out of sight, out of mind" would have kicked in.

On Saturday they'd talked long enough for Tessa to describe the family and her arrival in some detail, before she had reluctantly said she'd better get back to work.

Tonight, Sunday, Soon Heng offered a chair, but Tessa shook her head. She enjoyed the sensation of curling into a tight ball while she talked to Michael. Somehow it helped to calm her nerves.

"How'd it go today?" he said.

"We went to Sentosa. I tried to convince Soon Khim—that's the younger brother, the one who speaks English so well—not to do anything out of the ordinary, but it seems the family goes every two or three weeks. I got a lot of pictures; outside is always great."

"Doing what?"

"Roller skating."

"You as well?" She sensed his smile. "I'd like to have seen you do that."

"Especially juggling three cameras and a backpack."

"You didn't!"

She laughed. "You're right, I didn't. Terra firma for me."

A pause, and she searched for a new topic. "How was church?"

"Jillian came. She hated it."

"I'm sorry."

"There's hope. She said she'd read the New Testament, and that's better anyway. She'll meet Christ best through the Word."

Best maybe, but also through Michael.

"You know, about Jillian…" Michael paused. "You probably realize she's going through a hard time."

Yes, but why?

This time she kept her mouth shut, hoping he'd explain.

He didn't: "What are your plans for tomorrow?"

"Shopping in the morning with the grandmother, Soon Ah Lan, then over to the boys' day care/preschool center to photograph them at lunch, followed by school in the afternoon with Ah Mooi, and then back to the day care in time to catch Mui Chin picking the boys up."

"Mui Chin's the younger woman."

"Mei Ah Koh's niece."

"Just trying to keep everyone straight. You sound tired. Are you getting enough sleep?"

Tessa laughed. "This is five-star compared to some places I've worked."

"Where's your bed?"

"I sleep in the same room as Mui Chin and Soon Ah Lan and Ah Mooi. They have a cot set up for me in the corner."

"But you stay up until the last people go to bed, right? And make yourself get up as soon as anyone does?"

"It's only for seven days."

"True." He cleared his throat, and when he spoke again he sounded a little diffident. "Shall I call tomorrow?"

"Yes." She realized, panicked, that he could very easily decide not to. "Please do, Michael. I...look forward to it, really."

And on that note, now before he hung up...She pushed her hair back from her forehead and winced. Oh, well—

"Would you do something for me, Michael? I know you think I'm crazy, but about Blake—can you find out how well they checked him out before hiring him? His references, for example, and if they personally talked to anyone he worked with."

He grunted. "You're really worried about this."

"I am, Michael, and I'm not given to premonitions, truly, or silly, groundless worries. There's something—I don't know, but if they did a thorough enough background search, if everything checked out, then I could stop worrying, couldn't I?"

"I don't know."

"Please, Michael."

"All right, I can try."

"But without him knowing. That's *really* important."

"I'll see what I can do."

This time he didn't hesitate. After a quick good-bye, he hung up.

Tessa folded her cell phone and tapped it lightly against her mouth. He thought she was nuts. She could tell. Obsessed and ridiculous—just the way she was about her photography.

Just the way she was beginning to be about him, a little voice whispered—all over again, four years notwithstanding.

She sighed. Time to go in.

"Well, how's life in Marine Parade's five-star hotel?" Michael said Monday night.

"Very filling! Really, Michael, they eat all the time. I mean, not *all* of them all the time, but someone all the time. Tonight, for example, I got home with Mui Chin and the boys. We went into the kitchen almost immediately where Soon Ah Lan had a beef dish ready. I took some pictures of her feeding the younger boy, Ah Kheng. Mei Ah Koh—the mother—appeared and ate with us until she had to leave for a meeting. Soon Heng didn't get home from the orchid farm until seven-thirty. And then Soon Khim arrived home from the television station at nine, ready to eat his share.

"So much was happening in the kitchen that I finally took my computer in there to transfer caption notes. But every time someone new came in, Soon Ah Lan would give them their food, and they'd all say the same thing: 'Join me?' I think it's etiquette. No matter what anyone's eating, they have to make the invitation: 'Join me?' They didn't seem to care that I'd already eaten, not even Soon Ah Lan who was there the whole time, serving up the food. She kept filling my bowl again, and wouldn't you know it, down it went, easy as ice cream. I'm absolutely stuffed."

"The grandmother sounds like an all-around treasure."

"Soon Ah Lan. She is, Michael. This morning she gathered

everyone's dirty clothes and washed them all in a tiny electric washing machine that she hooks up to the sink in the kitchen. Then she strung them onto a bamboo pole and stuck them out the window to dry."

"Everyone's—yours included?"

"She offered and somehow I found myself accepting. She's like that; you just can't say no. We went shopping then, Soon Ah Lan shuffling down all three flights of stairs—I got great pictures in the market. I had to leave then, to get to the boys' preschool, but when I got home she had ironed everything, my clothes included. The apartment, of course, looked spotless."

"Any other good pictures?"

"Wonderful ones, all day."

"You sound excited."

"Do I? I'll try to calm down."

"Tessa! Enjoy yourself. I'm glad things are working out."

"Sometimes it happens that way. The angles are there; the background works out. But honestly, Michael, this family makes it easy. They do love each other, all contingent on the grandmother, I think. She's the peg that grounds them, though I doubt she considers what she does sacrifice. She has this tremendous contentment and satisfaction in her life."

Michael laughed. "Let me guess—she's Buddhist."

"Oh, Michael!" Tessa clapped a hand over her mouth. "You're right, she is. Is that where it comes from?"

"You're closer to the situation than I am, so you would know better. It's probably a combination of a lot of things. Her Buddhism, yes, and temperament and training and good examples, all aided by her Confucian background. There's much to value in Confucian thought, not the least being that she sees her family's success as her own and has taught her children to provide the same commitment and interest to each other."

"But, Michael…" Tessa frowned. "How can you discount Buddhism when the results are so admirable?"

"On the principle that the ends justify the means?"

"Michael!"

"Okay, okay." He cleared his throat. "I discount Buddhism first because I believe the God of the Bible exists and that it's right for him to receive our praise and gratitude. However admirable the results of Buddhist thinking, Soon Ah Lan can't please God because she does her good deeds with the wrong intent, to please herself."

"That sounds so harsh."

"What you're asking about goes to the very heart of why we are here. We exist for him, Tessa, for his pleasure."

And because of that Soon Ah Lan would be lost?

What if she and Michael had it all wrong, and the true God of the universe took whatever praise or worship people offered, regardless of religious trappings? Maybe God handed out truth in parcels, a portion here, a portion there, so that no one religion had it all.

"But does she have to do everything under the name of Christianity?"

"Tessa," he countered, "it's Jesus who said it: 'No one comes to the Father except through me.' I can't jettison the claims that he himself made and still call myself a Christian."

"But people do!"

"If all we needed were rules for good living, any of these religions would do—Buddhism, Hinduism, Islam. But Jesus does more than provide a good role model. Go back to the cross and what he accomplished there. It can never be duplicated: the satisfaction of God's holy requirements, the appeasing of his wrath, the hope of a relationship we can never know except through his death. Reconciliation, remember? Cessation of hostilities, not just tranquility. It's a *relationship* he saved us for, and we can't have that with a holy God except through Jesus Christ."

"But they're such good, good people," she said. "If you only saw how lovingly they treat each other."

He made a sympathetic sound low in his throat. "Prayer, Tessa. That's your source of hope. And *you*. Maybe God brought you into their lives so that he could bring himself in as well."

She pressed her face against the metal railing along the balcony. As late as it was, people still moved around, sat on benches and talked, played basketball, walked their dogs. So many, many people, multiplied a hundred, a thousandfold throughout the world, and day after day, insistent and closed-minded and absolutely unwilling to bend their hearts to the only One who could save them. The railing seemed suddenly like prison bars, the truth confining and unbearable.

"Don't despair," Michael said. "God will do what is *right*."

Down below, a small child, awake far beyond a sensible bedtime, ran into a man's arms. He threw the child up into the air, and though too distant to hear, Tessa imagined the sound of happy laughter.

Would he? she wondered bleakly. Really? *Completely* right?

Her shoulders sagged. "I better go back in."

"You're sounding tired again."

"Yes, I suppose I am."

But not so much physically this time.

"You'll call me, won't you," he said, "if you want to talk? Anytime. You have my number at the bank."

"I'm okay, Michael, really. Thanks for calling."

~ ~ ~ ~ ~

By Tuesday night, the Soon family had begun to wait for Michael's call to Tessa.

"Michael, they'd like to meet you." Tessa smiled at the grinning faces around her. "Are you free Saturday evening for dinner at a restaurant?"

"I won't get to sample Soon Ah Lan's cooking?"

She laughed and covered the receiver. "I've told him about your cooking, Soon Ah Lan. He says he'll be very sorry to miss the chance to sample it."

Smiling, Soon Khim translated, sending Soon Ah Lan into embarrassed giggles. She waved her hand back and forth in front of her face and shook her head.

"She says, no, no," Soon Khim explained. "A banquet will be much better."

Tessa bowed slightly to indicate the choice was Soon Ah Lan's, then excused herself. "You said it yourself," she told Michael, once she had reached the privacy of the balcony. "This isn't exactly the kind of house an expatriate banker finds himself visiting."

"Too bad. After hearing so much about them, I'd certainly like to visit them at home."

He would, Tessa thought, because he wasn't a typical expatriate. Just as Pastor Keenan had said.

"I'm sorry," she said. "I doubt I can change their minds. They began planning the banquet last Saturday."

"I see—in your honor. It didn't take them long to make up their minds about you."

Tessa laughed. "They're easy to like. They would have felt the same about any photographer."

"Maybe. So what have you been up to today?"

Tessa grinned. "Remember I said they eat all the time?

176

Tonight they seemed to all arrive home fairly early, around seven I think. The two men, Soon Heng and Soon Khim, went downstairs after supper to talk with their friends, but they soon came back up asking for spring rolls. Ah Mooi joined in, begging for Long John Silver's, and before you know it, off they all went to buy both. They're sitting around the television now, still chowing down, except for Soon Heng—that's the father, remember—who's gone off on some mysterious mission. Oh—look at that. Just a minute, Michael."

She slipped inside, offered excuses for walking in front of the television, and came back to the balcony with her tripod and camera.

"Are you still there?" she said. "I just have to get this shot. Soon Khim, the macho younger brother, is sitting on a stool, holding the little boy, Ah Kheng, asleep in his arms, with Ah Mooi, the five-year-old daughter, leaned up against his other shoulder, getting very drowsy."

"Are you taking the picture through the balcony door?"

"No." She adjusted the focus. "I have the door open just a little bit. Fortunately, Soon Khim's engrossed in the program. There! This picture will secure his romantic future. He looks so manly, you know, great muscles, and dressed in low-slung pajamas and a sleeveless undershirt, but it also shows his tender side."

"Best shot of the day?"

"Yes, maybe, if it turns out."

"Who'd you follow today?"

"Mei Ah Koh, the wife and mother, who teaches in a high school, from the time she woke up, all the way through her day. I got a wonderful shot of her at the kitchen table after school, bouncing the little boy Ah Kheng with one arm while trying to grade papers with the other."

"Not exactly career woman bliss."

"He was crying. I don't know if he was tired or wanted something to eat from Soon Ah Lan or what, but I did manage one shot—and only one—before Soon Ah Lan saw what I was doing and whisked Ah Kheng away."

"It may not have been you. Chinese babies are rarely allowed to cry for long."

"The other winner, then, was Ah Mooi making her case for Long John Silver's—a classic pouty face. In one, if the lighting works out, I think I got her father scolding her back—lots of personality there, with Soon Khim in the background, playing the amused bachelor uncle."

"You know," Michael said, "I can hardly wait to see these pictures."

She hung up soon afterwards, but stayed on the balcony, reliving the conversation. It really might work, this kind of friendship. She hugged herself. And surely he didn't seem quite so resentful of her photography?

The only disappointment was Blake. She'd meant to ask about him. Yet somehow, while she was talking with Michael, Blake seemed the lesser threat; offending Michael, the greater.

But she *would* ask tomorrow.

"Michael, I hope I'm not interrupting you."

"No. I'm having a sandwich at my desk today. Where are you? Is something wrong?"

"Everything's fine. I'm in a taxi on my way to Soon Khim's television station. He's taking me to lunch if he can get away. I just wanted to tell you what Soon Heng's mysterious mission was last night. I'll give you a hint. Skunks smell sweet in comparison."

"Ah." Michael chuckled. "Durians."

"Yes, exactly—those spiky little balls of stench masquerading as fruit. When he walked in the door, you would have thought he had just returned from the wars. They all jumped up and rushed to greet him, even Soon Ah Lan who never does more than shuffle, ever. *They* headed toward the door; I took one whiff and headed straight to the *balcony.* That smell is unbelievable."

He laughed again. "It's a Singapore joke, you know, that if God had put durians in the Garden of Eden, Eve would never have been tempted, and we'd all be sitting prettier now."

"I believe it! Tell me quick, have you ever eaten any? This one smelled like an open sewer."

"Or worse."

"Have you?"

"Yes," he said. "Three times."

"And…?"

"Three times was definitely *not* the charm for me. Maybe four."

"You are a brave soul. Whoops, here's Soon Khim's building."

"Just one question," Michael said. "Did you get any pictures?"

"Two, but I doubt they were any good. It was like having a fatal error on the computer. All my senses blinked out."

He was still laughing as she hung up.

"Hope it's not too late," Michael said Wednesday evening. "My Bible study went a little long tonight."

"That's okay—ooph." Tessa winced as she sat down. A pillow tonight might have helped.

"What's the matter? Sit on something sharp?"

"Hardly. I'm paying the price for being a major klutz. I

slipped on a playground unit at Ah Mooi's school today—that's Soon Heng and Mei Ah Koh's five-year-old daughter, in case you're still having trouble keeping the names straight. I had the perfect angle. She was playing below with her friends, having such fun. But right in the middle of the shot, I leaned out a little too far on the jungle gym, and went over. Not all the way—I managed to keep my legs gripped—but I swung down pretty hard and hit a metal bar."

"I suppose your equipment's okay?"

He said it dryly, so that she knew he was chiding her. "Why, Michael, you're beginning to think like a photographer."

"Where did you hit?"

"Fortunately I had taken off my backpack. But I could have dropped the camera I was holding."

"Tessa!"

"Oh, all right—the small of my back, but don't worry. It's only bruised."

"I suppose," he said, "we can all be relieved that you haven't decided to specialize in war zone pictures."

Tessa giggled. "It did cause quite a stir on the playground, though. They thought I must be some kind of circus performer when I climbed up there in the first place, and then when I started doing daring deeds—well, they were quite disappointed when I wobbled back down, a mere mortal."

"I imagine the teacher had no idea what to do with you."

Tessa laughed. "I don't think I'll try going back. I'm afraid she wouldn't let me in."

"Mmm."

He sounded sympathetic. But for Tessa or the teacher? She grinned.

"Oh!" She sat up straighter against the railing. "I have found an absolutely wonderful idea for a feature photographic spread. Walking up and down the stairs here in the housing unit, I've had a chance to notice the way people decorate their doorways. They're an incredible sociological object lesson."

"What do you mean?"

Afraid she was babbling, she nevertheless pressed on. "They identify so much about the family that lives there, especially what's important to them. Taoist trigrams, for example, and yin-yang emblems. Portraits of Jesus and Mary. Guru Nanak's portrait—he's the Sikh prophet, you know, of that sect in India. And there are Islamic quotations and pictures on the doors of the Chinese goddess Kwan Yin. The Hindu families string mango leaves across their doors, and I saw more than one with a picture of Lord Ganesh. He's the blue elephant god with the big trunk."

"And you noticed all these as you walked up three flights of stairs?"

Tessa laughed self-consciously. "Mui Chin and I walked around after supper with Ah Chye and Ah Mooi. I couldn't take any pictures of the doors at the time because the film in my camera belongs to Asia Premier, but don't you think it would make a great spread?"

"Or perhaps a poster like the one I've seen with the doors of outhouses in Europe."

"That's a great idea, Michael. Such a good way to represent Singapore. Maybe Ivy would be interested." She heard the rush in her voice and pressed her lips together. "I'm probably boring you."

"Not at all," Michael said. "Our phone conversations have been the best part of my week."

"It's been a bad one?"

"Very typical. Meetings, calculations, phone conferences, and more meetings. Reports, more calculations, and more meetings."

"Um..." She gathered her courage. "In between all that routine, did you find out anything about Blake?"

"Ah, Blake. Yes, I did, in fact. Without naming anyone, I asked someone in personnel how thoroughly they checked out employees before hiring them." Michael made an ironic sound. "He said very thoroughly for local employees, hardly at all for officers like me and Blake and Jillian. For us, they rely on the headhunters they hire through—their reputation's at stake, after all. Though they do call references, he said, and do a few other cursory checks."

"And how about a résumé? Have you seen Blake's?"

"I tried, Tessa. Remember, we talked about it coming back from the chemical plant? It won't work. His files are confidential. I do know he's from Tennessee, and he's worked in several reputable banks in the Midwest before coming here."

"Isn't there someone you could call, someone who might have known him?"

He paused. She could sense his reluctance.

"Michael, please."

"Let me get back to you on that."

As in, *drop it if I don't.*

What did he think, that she was worried on her own account? She'd be out of Singapore in a few weeks. It was Michael who would have to face the consequences, if she was right about Blake. "You did say, better a little precaution?"

"These aren't mixing tanks at a chemical plant, empty drums, or control boards. This is a man's life you're talking about, his reputation. I can't start putting that at risk on a whim."

"Fine." She sighed. "I'd better get back in."

And that was that.

The next night, Thursday, still feeling foolish, Tessa asked what Michael had been doing that evening.

"Soccer, of course, and then I came back to the office to finish up some work."

"You're there now?"

"As we speak."

She pictured him at his desk. Would he be wearing his soccer clothes, or had he returned to his apartment to change? "What did you have for supper?"

"Chicken and rice and a green bean dish. Mrs. Ling's cooking."

So he *had* gone back.

"How was the game?"

"Wonderful." She pictured him leaning back in his chair, grinning, perhaps even propping his feet up on his desk if no one else was there. "I put a little boy named Gavin in as goalie the second half, fairly new, just moved to Singapore with his parents. He easily stopped the first shot on goal. 'What do I do now?' he says to me—I'm back by the goal this time. 'Pick up the ball,' I tell him, 'run a ways, and kick it.' Well, he ran all right—all the way down the field, him at the front, Gary charging along after him, and all the rest of the kids racing along behind. Gavin must have thought the parents screaming on the sideline were cheering him on. He made it almost to the other end before Gary managed to catch up with him."

"I wish I'd been there to see it."

"Me too. It's that kind of exuberance, pure, unadulterated enthusiasm, that will keep me doing this for years."

Years?

Scenes of Michael on a soccer field stretched before her, year after year, until one day it would be his own children, his own little girl, whom he picked up and cuddled.

And who, she wondered, would be watching, like Carol, on Michael's sideline?

"Anyway," she heard him say, "how were the pictures today?"

She gathered her strength. "Bad. I followed the father, Soon Heng, to his orchid farm, but as you know it rained off and on all day. He went out anyway, of course, and so did I, but the lighting's always a little tricky on days like this, and it just didn't seem to be clicking—pardon the pun."

"Perhaps tomorrow?"

"I should have gone with him on Tuesday, which was a nice sunny day, instead of with his wife, Mei Ah Koh. I could photograph inside the high school in any weather." Tessa shrugged. "But, yes, I'll try again tomorrow, early in the morning. But things got even worse as the day progressed. While I was with Soon Heng, Ah Mooi—the little girl—threw up at school, and Soon Ah Lan had to go get her. They should have called me! It's such a classic family event—dealing with a sick child. And by the time I did get home, Ah Mooi was fine, of course, running around like normal, the whole thing finished."

"How disappointing," Michael said.

He sounded very earnest...*too* earnest.

"She definitely should have stayed sick until you got there," he continued sagely. "Um, what part of her getting sick *exactly* did you want to catch on film?"

"You're no help at all," Tessa said. "At times like this, you're supposed to nod and commiserate and be very, very sympathetic."

He laughed. "I'll try to remember that. So, tomorrow? What besides the orchid farm?"

"I'll spend the rest of the morning with the older boy, Ah Chye, in his preschool—"

"No playground shots, I hope."

She made a face. "And then catch an afternoon with Mui Chin at the university. She says she picks the boys up early every Friday and takes them on an outing—the zoo this week."

"No kidding? I wonder, shall I meet you there?"

"Really? You mean...to watch me?"

"If it wouldn't make you too nervous."

"Of course not. I'd like you to come. You can be my assistant for the afternoon."

"Oh? And what does an assistant do?"

"Carry things, of course! And if you learn very fast, you can hand me lenses and filters and things like that."

"Count me in, then. What time shall I be there?"

"Three o'clock, at the entrance."

Feeling like a child on Christmas Eve, Tessa sat a little longer on the balcony after he hung up. She was looking forward to seeing him—though she still wasn't sure about this "just friends" thing. Her usual solution to problems, she was beginning to realize, was to press on to the next big assignment. Work she could manage, keep on a tight rein, know where she stood. People were a greater risk. With them she maintained only the loosest of ties, and if knots developed— which they usually did—distance severed the bond neatly.

She tipped her head back against the balcony railing. She'd have a chance soon enough to see how her usual scheme worked with Michael. Next week, she'd be in Mumbai, the two weeks after in Australia. That should be a nice test of distance.

FOURTEEN

A call from Kuala Lumpur delayed Michael the next afternoon so that he had to go into the zoo to find Tessa. Though it was still a weekday, enough people filled the walkways for Michael to wonder if he might not find her. Given her story about the playground, he began looking up into the trees that lined the zoo area, but all the climbing creatures he saw seemed to belong there.

On the same principle, he began looking for a crouching figure and in this way found her photographing some children in front of the monkey display. Along with her White Sox cap, she wore shorts and a T-shirt, and heavy hiking boots. He understood the cap now. It certainly did help to camouflage her blond hair, if not her age. She looked far too young to be so accomplished in her profession.

Though she had straps for three cameras around her neck, he saw only one, then realized she had tucked the other two into a soft leather bag over one shoulder. Less noticeable, he decided, and she could exchange the cameras easily enough when she needed to. She carried the bigger Eastpak backpack as designed, on her back.

She stayed on her haunches, duck-stepping from one side to another, but taking all the shots from a low angle. He soon figured out her thinking. Built on an open-moated concept, the Singapore Zoo used either dry or wet ditches to separate animals from people. By crouching, Tessa was able to shoot above the narrow water-filled moat between her and the spider monkeys, making it look almost as if the children were playing among them.

He wondered, with sudden humor, if she knew how stiff the fine would be for jumping across the moat herself to get a better angle. Perhaps even Tessa realized she couldn't go that far.

She stood and saw him. "Michael, here you are. Mui Chin, this is Michael Lawton, the one who's been calling me all week."

The young Singaporean woman had straight black hair, cut simply at her shoulders, a flawlessly smooth complexion, and bright, curious eyes. She gave Michael a quick smile. "I am pleased to meet you."

Two boys were pressing close against her legs. She glanced down and smoothed the younger boy's hair back from his forehead.

"And this is Ah Chye and Ah Kheng," Tessa said.

"Are you enjoying the zoo?" Michael asked the boys.

Ah Chye, the older, held back, but Ah Kheng nodded his head vigorously.

"Then, please," Michael said, directing this statement to Mui Chin, "don't let me interrupt you."

"As I told you, Mui Chin, Michael will be serving as my assistant today," Tessa said. She passed her backpack over to Michael with a smile. "You and the boys please go ahead and enjoy the zoo as you normally would."

Michael hefted the bag over his shoulder. "This is it? Nothing more for the beast of burden?"

"It'll become burden enough before we're done, trust me."

The younger boy, Ah Kheng, said something in Chinese. He had said it earlier. This time he sounded close to meltdown.

"What does he want to see?" Tessa asked Mui Chin.

"The Komodo dragon. It's at the reptile house…which is where we go lah." The latter part of her statement she directed to Ah Kheng.

After a quick change to another camera and a slide to the left, Tessa crouched again in time to catch Mui Chin being dragged by Ah Kheng with one hand while she beckoned to Ah Chye with her other.

"Do you think that one will turn out?" Michael said, as they hurried after them.

"Maybe, though with so many elements it's hard to know, and I only managed the one shot."

"What do you mean?"

"The angle of Ah Kheng's body tugging forward, whether enough of Mui Chin's face showed to catch her expression, if Ah Chye still hadn't started moving when I took the picture. If it works, it will certainly show a lot about family dynamics. Ah Kheng's energetic and quick; Ah Chye more careful and methodical."

They skirted the giraffe display, somewhat eerie since nothing but a trench only three feet deep encompassed their home.

"We are very proud of our zoo," Mui Chin said, speaking more formally for Michael's benefit. "Few zoos feel ready to make the financial investment necessary for an open-moat system, but Singapore Zoo grows slowly, adding a little bit, little bit."

"I would imagine the system requires a lot more space than cages," Michael said, "but how wonderful to see the animals like this."

Mui Chin nodded quickly.

The ten-foot Komodo dragon lizard, when they arrived at the Reptile House, impressed even Michael. But it wasn't until they had reached Children's World, with its domesticated animals, that Tessa began photographing again. Mui Chin had picked up a baby chick for Ah Chye to pet.

"Oh, dear," Tessa said. She removed a lens, thrust it into Michael's hand, and reached for another out of the backpack.

Then she moved in very close. Michael thought she must be photographing only their hands, overlapping in the fuzzy yellow feathers.

After a week in front of the lens, the boys and Mui Chin hardly noticed the camera. They trusted Tessa, Michael realized. Perhaps that, even more than the artistic eye, was the great gift she brought to photography.

"I'd sure like to see these," he told her as they made their way back to the zoo's entrance.

"A courier's been coming every day to pick up the film. Ivy's called a couple of times to say they're turning out well."

"Will she go through them with you, to show which ones she's chosen?"

"I might even have a say in what's selected, though who knows?" She grinned. "This being Singapore and all."

"When you do that, could you pass me off as your assistant? I'd love to go along."

"'Pass you off?' Given Ivy's interest last Saturday," Tessa said, "she'd probably be glad to arrange a private viewing."

It was good to hear her teasing him. "And what," he followed that up with, "do you hear these days from Corin?"

She laughed. "Corin's doing just fine, thank you. He's in his element, I'm sure: dirty, sweaty, stinky, and stressed. No playground sets for him. Only real threats will do." She shrugged. "He'll be down in Indonesia for another five weeks at least."

"By then, you'll have finished here."

"Yes. I have a few weeks free after Australia. I'll probably head back to the States then, touch base with my agent, see what he's managed to line up for me next."

"Do you ever worry about getting more work?"

"Not as long as I keep taking what's offered—one job leads to another. Why?"

"Just curious." It certainly explained why she was so driven.

They continued walking, their pace set by the tired boys. As had happened so often during the past three weeks, Michael felt a familiar frustration creep over him, a slowly building despair. Her time in Singapore hadn't gone according to plan. Too little time together, too many interruptions, too little chance to win her over. And Jillian hadn't helped. He wished he could have followed Tessa all week, handing her lenses, carrying her pack, learning what she needed until he could anticipate her requests. Now her departure loomed.

"Bombay's first, though," he said. "When does that start?"

"I leave Monday morning. This assignment ends at twelve on Saturday—no more pictures after that. But I hope you're still planning on dinner with the Soons. Seven o'clock at the East Ocean restaurant in Shaw Centre. Do you know it?"

They had arrived at the entrance. Mui Chin was waiting with the boys.

"I'll pick you up at six-thirty," Michael said, "and we'll go together."

He watched her climb onto the bus after the others, then waited until it pulled away, trying not to see in her departure a premonition of what was to come.

Jillian called Tessa on her cell phone later that evening, shortly before eleven. "I suppose you were expecting Michael," Jillian said, after Tessa had retreated to a quiet spot in the kitchen. "Surprise! It's me. I hope it's not too late. Michael thought it might be."

"It's okay. You sound a lot happier tonight."

"Believe me, I *am*. I'm feeling *great*. I could probably float down from the seventieth floor of the Weston Stamford, I feel so light, which is where we were tonight, by the way, on the seventieth floor, celebrating. Michael took me to eat filet mignon at the Compass Rose—he's been great—and then I badgered him into taking me on down to Sago Street to look at all the Chinese funeral stuff. Don't think I'm awful, but I just couldn't resist. They have paper Mercedes, paper servants, paper dishwashers and refrigerators, even a paper Boeing 747. It's all to bury with people so they have something with them in the world of the dead."

"It sounds like…quite an evening."

"You do think I'm awful. So did Michael. He was appalled. But I just couldn't resist, not tonight. Such perfectly *perfect* black humor, don't you think?"

Tessa was confused. Why would Jillian think she'd be appalled by a mention of funeral items—folk art, one travel book described them? She had been curious herself about seeing them. And why would Michael care?

"Anyway," Jillian was saying, "given the last few weeks, I just wanted to say I'm feeling great—thanks for your concern. And I'm looking forward to having you back."

After Jillian hung up, Tessa stared across the cramped space of the kitchen to the shelves lined with spices and dried mushrooms and other Teochew cooking ingredients. She must be more tired than she thought. Nothing Jillian had said made sense except that she had gone out with Michael to the Compass Rose and eaten filet mignon.

She stared at the phone and then carefully, deliberately, punched in his number.

"Tessa. I was afraid it might be too late to call."

"No, they're all up late tonight, which means we better not talk very long."

Would he mention Jillian? Would he ask if she had called?

Nothing.

"Thank you for coming to the zoo with me," she said.

"I enjoyed it."

No doubt. And then you went from there to a cozy celebration with Jillian.

She rubbed her eyes. He must have been worried about her, that's why he kept calling. He thought this was *her* hard time, and he should support her. That's all it had been.

"Are you all right, Tessa?"

She pressed a palm against her forehead. She wasn't up to this now. "I better get back to work."

"See you tomorrow then."

She felt her shoulders sag. *That's right. Tomorrow.*

Tessa chased the yawns away with coffee, then stayed up later than usual with Soon Khim and Mui Chin, discussing everything from their opinion of Singapore's government to their experiences with the paranormal. They finally made it to bed around two in the morning, but even that late, Tessa couldn't sleep.

Partly, her muscles ached. Not sure how safe the Soons' locked cabinet would be against burglars, she had carried much of her equipment throughout the week. Adrenaline and ibuprofen masked the strain during work, but she felt it all now, along with the deep bruise at the small of her back. Every turn in bed produced a protest.

Even so, she didn't bother taking any more medication. It wasn't her aching body that was keeping her awake. It was Jillian's call. They had been "celebrating," Jillian said, and she felt "great." The exuberance in Jillian's voice still echoed in Tessa's mind.

She sat up on her little cot, rolled her shoulders several times, then slumped forward and put her elbows on her knees.

What could she do?

When she had first met him, fresh out of high school, she'd been irrationally attracted to his instinctive confidence and wit—attracted and confused. Never a girl to giggle over boys with her girlfriends, she had retreated into silence, and wasn't surprised later to discover that he had barely noticed her that first visit.

By the time she met him again six years later, she had traveled through much of the world and worked two years on a big-city newspaper, and she knew enough about men to welcome and even expect their attention. In Michael she found the complete package—attraction, kinship, common values and shared ideals, passion, laughter, and a mutual interest in many things. That he was also a Christian seemed like a nice bonus.

It *must* have been the same for him. He had proposed only three weeks later, after all.

And that was the problem, she supposed. They had gone too far, too fast, becoming engaged like that. Easy to cross from friendship to passion; so hard to go back.

She rubbed the muscles in her neck, wishing she could rub out her regret as easily. She knew *now* how precious—and necessary—a shared commitment to Christ was. She also knew now how rarely the complete package came along. In four years, no man had taken his place.

Utterly weary, she sank her head onto her hands.

She was beginning to doubt any man could.

She arrived at Jillian's apartment the next day to find that her yearbooks and her photo albums had arrived during the week. She made a face and pushed the package off the end of her bed. Michael wasn't concerned, so why should she be?

Anyway, Blake was a banker, wasn't he, and since when were bankers dangerous?

They could be obnoxious, yes, know-it-all and way too smart for the comfort of anyone around them, but *dangerous?*

She turned instead to her post-assignment work, organizing receipts for billing and tax purposes and totaling each day's expenses in her day book. She had been diligent about transferring caption notes and expenses onto the computer while at the Soons', so she finished fairly quickly. She took time as well during the afternoon to write to her father and her mother, crafting her messages carefully when referring to Michael, and then answered the other e-mail messages that had been piling up during her week with the Soons.

She also checked her equipment and packed her photo gear and clothes for the trip to Mumbai. Compared to photographing the Soon family, her time in India seemed pretty mild: two days in the city itself and two days travelling to outlying factories for photographs in situ. If everything went well, she'd be back in Singapore late Thursday afternoon.

Tessa left herself just enough time before dinner with the Soons to wash and dry her hair and slip into her lilac print dress. Standing at the mirror to put on makeup, Tessa winced at the soreness in her shoulder muscles. At the last minute, remembering Michael's reaction to her accident on the playground, she took one of her specially prescribed pain relievers.

The better to fool you with, Michael Lawton.

Jillian had been gone when Tessa came in earlier. She returned when Tessa was dressed. "You look great," she said from Tessa's bedroom door. "What a gorgeous dress. Want me to help with your hair?"

"I don't have time. Michael will be here any minute."

"Looks good anyway, and I'm late, too. I spent the whole

day shopping. It's good this kind of thing doesn't happen too often. The aftermath is getting expensive. I'll see you later."

The front door closed, leaving the effect of sudden silence after a megadecibel music performance. Tessa smiled. A rock concert, she decided, with a sassy female vocalist who had unlimited energy and lots of zing.

She put the hairbrush down. What then had been going on during the last two weeks? And what had brought that zing back again now?

Michael arrived within minutes. "I passed Jillian downstairs. She looked good."

Tessa almost laughed. *Jillian* did? Talk about leading with a big foot in mouth.

Feeling quite magnanimous—probably because of the painkiller—Tessa smiled benignly and let Michael get away with his faux pas. "She seems to be in a much better mood than when I left."

"No doubt."

Tessa paused, hoping he would respond to the ever-so-slight question she had put into her voice, but he merely pulled the door open for her and held out his hand. "We'd better go, or we'll be late."

In fact, they arrived at the East Ocean Restaurant right on time.

"If we'd come early," Michael informed Tessa, "we might have appeared too eager."

"But I *am* hungry!" Tessa objected.

"Behave," Michael said, but he was smiling.

When she preceded Michael into the small private room set aside for the Soon family, everyone clapped. Familiar with the procedure, Michael clapped back. No one had been sitting yet, waiting for Tessa and Michael to appear so that everyone could be seated in order of importance.

Everyone had come, it seemed, even the children. Tessa introduced Michael and then, feeling as if she were sharing a special treasure with him, introduced each of the people around the table. "And Mui Chin, of course, you met yesterday."

Soon Heng, as principal host, indicated the place on his left for Tessa. "Guest of honor, Tessa Brooks. And here for you, Mr. Lawton, my right side, please." Soon Heng went on to seat everyone else, beginning with his mother on the other side of Tessa and ending with Ah Kheng facing him with his back toward the door. Soon Heng sat down last.

From her research Tessa knew how carefully orchestrated the seating at a formal Chinese banquet was. By tradition, the guest always sat facing the door, in case an enemy appeared, and the host beside him, ready to defend him as well.

Again according to protocol, Soon Heng apologized for the poor food they would be eating, its insignificance, the meagerness of the display. From across the table, Michael caught Tessa's eye and smiled. Soon Heng's speech continued, followed by applause, and then he lifted his glass and invited everyone to drink. In this, too, tradition must be served. Everyone at the table, Michael and Tessa included, lifted their glasses first with their left hand, then slid the fingers of their right hand under the bottom of the glass, and drank.

Again Tessa looked across at Michael and was rewarded with an encouraging smile.

Following the drink, Soon Heng called for the first dish, a plate of thinly sliced cold meats. He served Tessa himself and then invited everyone else to eat. Tessa gave a silent sigh of relief. The meal had finally begun.

The dishes kept coming, chosen to balance spicy with bland, delicate with more flavorful, soft-textured foods with crispy. Teochew food, Tessa knew, in which both East Ocean and Soon Ah Lan specialized, prided itself in delicate seasoning that preserved and enhanced the natural flavorings. Several dishes were steamed—lobster, fish, and chicken—and quite bland. But some were more distinctive, including the fried liver rolls. Consisting of minced liver and water chestnuts, wrapped, deep-fried, and covered with a sweet soy molasses, they were surprisingly good. Soon Heng, who had undoubtedly chosen the menu, had included several specialties: sea cucumber stuffed with pork and spices, turtle soup, and abalone.

("I try to forget while I'm eating it," Michael told Tessa in the taxi home, "that sea cucumber is really just a sea slug."

"Better than thousand-year eggs," Tessa shot back, shuddering. "I can't eat those, no matter how hard I try.")

Throughout the dinner, between friendly conversation and the many courses, Soon Heng called for more toasts, and Tessa was relieved that Michael had earlier requested soft drinks for them both. A practiced guest, Michael exclaimed frequently over the dishes, praising Soon Heng's choices, praising the chef, praising the variety. And since he spoke so knowledgeably about Singaporean food in general and the subtle flavors of the dishes served in particular, he thoroughly impressed the Soon family.

When everyone stood, Tessa found herself immensely proud of both Michael and the Soons. The meal had been fun. The whole week had been fun, in fact, and she felt blessed to have brought two such divergent aspects of her life together with such success.

How different from the first meal she had shared with the

Soons the week before. Somehow, in the course of a week, they had brought her into their circle, ignoring the camera that usually caused such an impenetrable barrier between Tessa and the people she photographed.

And yet, for all their effort, would she ever see them again, ever even hear from them?

Perhaps because she knew the answer to this question, Tessa felt more regret than usual when she parted with the Soons. Michael must have sensed this. He remained mostly silent in the taxi home, and at Jillian's apartment, though it was still early, he declined an invitation to come in. "I'm sure you're still tired. Will you be coming to church tomorrow?"

"Of course."

"How's your bruise?" Very gently, he touched the base of her back. "I forgot all about this yesterday at the zoo."

"Well..." She scrunched up her nose, though for the sake of his concern, she might have been glad to do it all over again.

"That bad, huh?"

"A necessary drawback to the job, Michael. You must have something similar to it in banking." She looked him up and down. "Misaligned vertebrae from carrying a briefcase all the time? Or maybe your glasses, from having to read all that fine print."

"Sure. Hazards everywhere." Humor sparkled in his eyes. "That's banking for you."

"Well," she said, crossing her arms, "how many jobs require you to eat sea slug on a regular basis?"

He laughed outright. "Now there you do have a point."

Their smiles held.

A triumph, she told herself, as she pushed the door of Jillian's apartment shut between them. An easy exchange between friends who knew how to amuse each other. Exactly what she had hoped God would help her accomplish.

She leaned her head briefly against the closed door. Why, then, did she feel so deflated?

She overslept badly the next morning. Michael's knocking finally woke her. By the time she put on a robe and got to the door, he was already walking away toward the elevator.

He turned back when she called his name.

"I should have known this would happen," she said. "I always crash after a big assignment."

"Sure you don't want to stay home?"

"No, not from church if I can help it. Go ahead, if you want. I can make it on my own."

He looked at his watch. "How long?"

"Ten minutes?"

"I'll make some coffee."

Feeling groggy, she went back into the bedroom and squinted at her hair in the mirror. It had looked fine last night for the Chinese banquet. Why was it refusing to lie flat now? She slipped into her periwinkle jumper and white tee, wet her hair down in the bathroom, then juggled hair dryer and mascara back in her bedroom.

She glared at the results. Civilization hardly seemed worth it. On some assignments, insurgent hair wouldn't have mattered.

"Fourteen minutes," Michael said when she entered the kitchen. "Not bad. Are you planning to wear shoes?"

She looked down in surprise, threw up her hands, and headed back to the bedroom. "Go ahead and pour my coffee," she called to him. "Use the disposable cups in the cabinet by the sink. I'll drink it in the taxi."

And then to top it all off, it started to rain just as they were about to step from the apartment building. Michael, the magic man, whipped open an umbrella big enough for them both, but even so she felt a little betrayed after all the effort she'd put into her hair.

"You probably didn't even notice Jillian wasn't there," Michael said.

"Oh?"

"She left a message on my machine yesterday evening. She and a friend decided to catch the ferry over to Desaru on the southeast coast of Malaysia—beaches mostly, with water sports and golf."

"When is she coming back?"

"Tonight. It's just a one-day excursion."

Tessa tipped her head toward the window. "Too bad about the rain then."

Michael waved off her concern. "This'll blow over in no time."

"Mm." She snuck a sideways look at Michael. Still no word on whether the friend was male or female. He certainly looked relaxed. Did that mean the friend was female? Or that he just didn't care?

"Sorry you had to rush," Michael said. "No photos today, I see."

She shook her head.

"Well, I hope you're free for lunch. I've arranged for us to eat with Pang Li Hua, a young Singaporean woman who accepted Christ about three years ago. You said you'd like to meet someone like her?"

She had indeed. How nice to find a resource so well connected in his church. He'd had little trouble, apparently, finding someone for Tessa to meet.

Through Sunday school she dwelt on this fact. How different from her own experience. Since beginning her travels as a nineteen-year-old college dropout, she had worshipped in a bamboo hut in the hills of Myanmar, storefront churches in Taiwan, a huge building in Korea, riverside gatherings in India, longhouses in Indonesia, a house church in the Philippines, a community room in a Hong Kong high-rise—the list went on and on. But always, like today, only as a visitor.

In comparison, Michael's experience, even as an expatriate with a limited tenure here in Singapore, seemed stable and nourishing—and very enviable. Like the song from *Cheers:* People were glad he came.

She responded to people's polite greetings after Sunday school, then followed Michael into the sanctuary. Was this the compulsion behind her worldwide church project, she wondered? An attempt to document and confirm the only church she had known in her adult life?

"Are you all right?" Michael said as the pastor and worship leader took their places.

She nodded and smiled and the service began.

FIFTEEN

After church Michael led Tessa to a young woman standing near the doorway. In her early twenties, the woman's most noticeable feature was her eyes—serious, watchful, and intelligent.

"Hello, Michael," she said and held her hand out to shake his.

"Thank you for meeting us, Li Hua. This is my cousin, Tessa Brooks. Tessa, this is Pang Li Hua."

The young woman shook Tessa's hand, smiled, and asked a polite question about how long Tessa had been in Singapore. After that she seemed reluctant to talk. Tessa considered herself adept at enticing conversation from people, but even she found Li Hua tough going. Why had Michael chosen such a reticent young woman?

The rain had indeed blown over, as Michael said it would. Before they went out into the heat, he announced that he had made reservations at the Long Jiang—"a Szechuan restaurant with a large buffet." He smiled at Li Hua. "I hope that will be okay."

"Yes, thank you."

Tessa's mouth began to water as soon as she breathed in the spicy, pungent smells inside the restaurant. With typical Chinese decor, the centerpiece of the Long Jiang was its buffet with Szechuan specialties: hot-and-sour soup, smoked duck, sesame chicken, General Tso's chicken, shark fin soup, and much more. The host led them to a small table, and then left them to go through the line. Sitting at the table with a full plate in front of her, Tessa could hardly wait for the others to join her so they could pray. Perhaps just one small piece of General Tso's chicken?

Everything about Pang Li Hua seemed so proper, Tessa was glad she had resisted temptation. Michael prayed, and they all started eating.

After a few minutes, Tessa turned to Li Hua. "Have you lived in Singapore all your life?"

"Yes. My father is in business. He runs a consortium of business ventures. My mother is a housewife."

A wealthy background. That explained her excellent English.

"Are you in school now?"

Li Hua glanced at Michael who said, "I haven't told her anything."

She turned back to Tessa. "I live with a family as a kind of mother's assistant in exchange for room and board. During school hours, when the children are away, I work in a florist's shop. I am learning to arrange flowers."

What about her parents? Aware of something odd, Tessa merely said, "How wonderful to work with flowers all day."

The stiff smile appeared again, and they all returned to eating, Michael and Tessa carrying most of the conversation.

After the meal, they left the restaurant and took a taxi to Fort Canning Park where they walked together for a while, then found a place to sit on the grass.

"I was hoping you would share your testimony with Tessa," Michael said to Li Hua. "Will you?"

Though she didn't look comfortable with the idea, Li Hua agreed: "Yes, if you want."

"I would love to hear how you were saved," Tessa said. "There's no better story anywhere, is there, than how God saved us?"

Li Hua, looking stiffer than ever, smiled. "I think you are right, though such a story often starts badly. I hope you will remember that as I speak." She coughed and began: "I am twenty-five years old, the only child of my parents. My father, as I said, is a successful businessman who could afford to send me to the best possible schools. It was always his dream for me to attend university here and then train to become a lawyer at the London School of Economics. At university, only the best grades would suffice, but I began to have trouble. During my third year, even after studying many hours, I was in danger of failing my exams. You can imagine how bad that would be. No London School of Economics, not even a university degree. My father..." She sighed. "I am his only daughter. He put all his hopes on me. Day after day, the situation worsened, until finally I considered suicide. This is not a rare thing for students, especially because of bad grades. I began to think it was my duty, that it was the only way I could retain even a little of my father's respect."

"How difficult for you," Tessa said.

Again the small smile, though this time it seemed a little more genuine. "A nightmare of the worst kind, it is true. I could not eat. I could not sleep. I became very sick. I—" She paused, closed her eyes, then plunged on. "I began hurting myself. Like this." And she demonstrated by scraping the edge of an imaginary knife down the soft side of her arm, from her wrist to her elbow. "Over and over again, not enough to draw blood, only enough to scrape. When the skin became raw, I moved on to my upper thighs and then to my stomach."

Tessa winced.

Seeing her reaction, Li Hua said, "Please forgive the unpleasantness of this admission. I relate these deeds only to demonstrate how desperate my circumstances were. Also, as you will see, it was through the marks on my arm that God first reached out to me. This happened about six weeks before exams. I intended to keep studying, take the exams, and if I failed, kill myself. I think now I would never have lasted that long. It is only a small flick of the hand, do you see, to move from scraping my skin to slicing my wrists."

Tessa sucked in a breath. No wonder Michael had waited until after they had finished eating.

"I was in class that day," Li Hua continued. "I looked down to discover that I had allowed the button on my cuff to fall off. I had nothing to pin it together again. I tried to hold it, but during the lecture, while I was taking notes, my sleeve fell down my arm, and the student next to me saw the scrapes. She felt only concern—she told me this later—but I was filled with fear. I imagined somehow she must know what I had been doing, and all was lost. My father would find out and put me in a hospital or an insane asylum, to his great shame and debasement. I stumbled out of class, went to the lavatory, and threw up. Joan Chiew—I did not know her name then—followed me, waited until I had finished, and then took me home with her."

"She was a Christian," Tessa said.

"She was Christ to me. Her hands applied his comfort. Her ears listened in his place. She fed me and worried over me and, though I did not know it at the time, prayed and prayed and prayed. Six weeks later, I did indeed pass the exams, but I knew even as I took them I would never study in London."

"Never?"

"Because by then I had become a Christian, and I knew my parents would disown me." She watched Tessa's reaction and then smiled. "You are surprised. You did not expect this?"

"I thought people in Singapore didn't care what you believe."

"Christians care," Li Hua said. "Would you not expect the same devotion from at least a few Buddhists?"

"You were a Buddhist?"

"My mother, my father, my grandparents, and all my ancestors. And that is the problem, do you see? Many Buddhists believe they will receive ritual veneration and care from their descendants. If I am a Christian, who will care for my parents?"

"You knew this when you became a Christian?"

"You are wondering, I suppose, if it affected my decision. Miss Brooks," Li Hua said quite firmly, "God came into my life at a time when I desperately needed him. Without Joan sitting beside me in class that day, without my button falling off, my sleeve sliding down, her look of concern, and my breakdown, without all these events and all of them in order, I might very well be dead today."

"I see that," Tessa said.

"And when Joan explained Christian belief to me, God made it so I understood immediately. I could not meet my *own* father's demands so I tried to pay for my failures—to suffer enough to make things right." She crossed her forearms, gripping them tightly. "Please understand, it was not a hardship doing this. It felt good. I was angry, terribly angry at myself— wrath is too small a word. And each stroke on my arm, each scrape and pain, released some of that anger, giving a little peace. But as you know, it was never enough. Death seemed the only conclusion. And then to learn that Jesus paid my penalty for me. After all that, I had no choice, no matter what my parents said. 'By his wounds'—is that not correct, Michael?"

He had been sitting about four feet away and a little sideways from them, not looking at Li Hua. He turned now and nodded, his eyes grave and sympathetic.

Li Hua held her arms out for Tessa to see. "I do not even

have scars, do you see—healed inside and out." She looked more relaxed now that her story was over, carefree in fact. She turned to Tessa and laughed. "My poor parents! I am a kiasu disaster in their eyes, the worst possible kind of failure, to go from such wealth to living as an unpaid servant in an HDB flat. But I do not mind. God is pleased, I know he is, and that means success for me now."

"Can't you go back to school? Isn't there anyone who can help you?" Without realizing what she was doing, Tessa shot a glance at Michael.

He shook his head, but before he could say anything, Li Hua laughed again and clapped her hands. "Do not malign your friend Michael, please. He has offered, but I will not take that road. Singapore is full of people who profess Christ to gain material benefits. Michael can tell you this is true. Let me be one example of the other—someone who gives up worldly benefits to serve Jesus."

Tessa, too moved to speak, squeezed Li Hua's hand.

"Please, do not look so sad," Li Hua said. "Humble yourself, the Bible tells me, and he will lift you up. I believe it. I have lost nothing and have gained my soul."

Tessa exchanged a quick look with Michael, smiled, then squeezed Li Hua's hand again. "I am not sad, just deeply moved. I told you. There's no better story in all creation."

Tessa and Michael walked Li Hua to the edge of the park afterwards, where they saw her off in a taxi. Tessa couldn't move at first, but could only stand watching down the road where the taxi had gone. When she lifted her eyes to Michael, she saw in them the same warm sympathy that he had shown Li Hua.

"What an amazing testimony," she said, then added, "What amazing grace. She's still estranged from her parents?"

"As if dead."

"How awful. I suppose I just assumed…I mean, I've heard of similar stories in India, but Singapore seems so advanced."

"Consider Li Hua herself, the strength of her convictions, the self-discipline, and determination. I imagine she gained those traits from her father."

"How do you know her?" Tessa said. "I don't suppose she tells this story to just anyone."

"You mean what do I have over her?" Michael laughed. "She was one of my students the first year I taught, then she decided she wanted to teach a similar course and came back again for another full year. She teaches a class for university students now."

"No kidding." Tessa looked again to where they had been sitting. "Thank you so much for arranging this, Michael."

"My pleasure."

The sounds of the park continued behind them. Michael stood beside Tessa on the sidewalk, looking a little distracted, or perhaps, uncertain.

"What now?" Tessa said. "Do you have work to do?"

"No. What about you? Do you need to finish packing for Mumbai?"

She shook her head. "I finished that yesterday."

"In that case—" He cleared his throat. "You said a while back you'd show me your worldwide church project."

"You mean, now?"

"If you don't mind."

She paused, suddenly reluctant. "We'll need to go back to Jillian's apartment."

He glanced at the sky. "Then we'd better hurry. It'll be raining again before we get there."

All week he had thought about this, worried that she might have work to finish from her assignment, be too tired, need to pack, and yet by his calculations, this was almost his last chance to see her hidden work.

At the door of Jillian's apartment, she paused. "You sure you have time for this?"

She was nervous? He bit back a smile. "Yes."

"Well, sit down then. I'll go get what I have." She took a step toward the bedroom, then hung back. "You must have an idea of what this project is."

This time he did smile. "I suppose, pictures of Christians from around the world?"

She nodded and disappeared, returning with three large albums. "Forgive my anxiety," she said. "I'm always nervous showing my work—terrified, in fact—but especially these pictures, since they're so close to my heart. But before I show you, can I ask you a question? How did you know I'd want to tour the petrochemical plant with you? It wouldn't be on most people's short list of places to visit in Singapore."

Whoops! He took off his glasses and started to clean them.

"Michael?"

"I seem to remember a discussion with your mother and my uncle about the many annual-report pictures you take and how unfortunate it was when the companies wouldn't let you submit any of the photographs to your stock agency."

"That means," she said and crossed her arms, "when I explained stock photography, you already knew all about it."

"I'd never heard *your* explanation, Tessa."

"Hmm. Well, thank you for arranging the tour anyway."

"My pleasure."

She looked in his direction, still a little confused.

He merely smiled.

"Okay," she said, "the worldwide church. I got this idea, believe it or not, from reading *Malcolm X*, the book about the African-American Muslim leader, as an extra-credit project in high school. Have you read it?"

He shook his head. "I've heard of him."

"In the book, when he goes to Mecca, he's amazed and impressed by the worldwide diversity of Islam. Every Islamic man is supposed to make the pilgrimage once in his life, so it's understandable that the group there at any given time includes people from throughout the world. I found myself envious, wishing Christians had a similar gathering. We have a multi-ethnic, multiracial church, too. It would be easier to remember that, don't you think, if we could see the different people God calls?"

High school. She had been thinking like this in *high school*.

"Once I began traveling," she said, "I regretted the lack of a worldwide church gathering even more."

"And you decided to make it possible through photography."

"It was all I had, and even that seemed hopeless when I first started. I expected to go back to college, you know, and then who knows how much chance I would have to travel."

"But now you have all these pictures?"

"Michael, I have hundreds of pictures, and those only after throwing out many hundreds more that I could never use. I bring these along," and she tapped the three albums on her lap, "to show to people whose permission I need for pictures, like Pastor Keenan. I have them divided into three groups: worship, ministry, and private moments."

He was itching for a look. Did she ever intend to open the albums? Not yet, apparently.

"Pictures of worship and ministry are easy," she continued.

"Ethnic clothes and surroundings make worship exciting. Variety of endeavors and sacrifice and sometimes even conflict make pictures of service and ministry important. It's the private moment pictures that are hardest to capture, and yet if I had to choose—which is unnecessary—I would think those moments bring God the greatest pleasure. The world measures value too often by fame, people watching, the cover story, the evening news, but heaven cheers the small acts of devotion, I'm convinced, done for his approval and his alone." She had been gripping her hands, the passion of her words finding physical expression there. She must have realized what she was doing because she let go and shook them out. "I'm getting carried away. I always do. I'm sorry."

"I don't mind." He took her hand in his and massaged the palm before returning it. "Do you have many of these private moment pictures?"

"Eleven. And every one a miracle. I rarely have a chance to bracket those pictures—I did explain bracketing, didn't I? Taking extra shots at different settings? Well, for those I usually have one chance and only one to get the shot, and yet every one has turned out well. That I have the opportunity at all is a gift from God."

"So…" He beckoned toward the books. "Let me see."

She winced and pushed the first album onto his lap. "Worship first."

Each page held an eight-by-ten-inch color print on one side with the caption opposite. As she had said, diversity of clothing and setting and nationality gave the pictures much of their appeal, though he easily saw the special touch Tessa added through the lighting and composition. She had managed somehow to superimpose unity over diversity through the common emotions seen on the people's faces—the joy in celebration, the quiet devotion, the reverent prayers, and the intent awareness as people listened.

Though many pictures featured corporate worship with people sitting in rows or circles, not all did. One extreme close-up revealed a mother's gentle hand showing her small son how to fold his hands for prayer. Another, a quick favorite for Michael, featured a bright, sunny Easter parade through an Indian village's main thoroughfare. A young girl, perhaps ten or twelve, walked beside a friend, holding her hand and laughing. In the background, Michael could see rows and rows of other people following behind, most of them singing, many of them excited, a few of them laughing like the girl.

"You've never sold these?" he said.

"I've considered it, once or twice, but I'd rather keep them all together." She wrinkled her nose. "The power's in the collection. I don't want to lose my punch."

He nodded. "I see what you mean."

Another series featured an Indian *mela,* the annual celebration that Christians from all over a region attended. Photographs showed spirited singing around a bonfire, speakers, meals eaten on the ground, Bible lessons, and the highlight of the event—the river baptism.

Tessa tapped her finger on the picture of a handsome youth coming up out of the water. The caption identified him as a high-born Brahmin, making the baptism a rare event. "Against people's advice," Tessa said, "he decided to return to his family after the *mela.* He was never seen again."

"Killed?"

"Poisoned, probably."

The young man's quietly joyful face dominated the photograph. Had he known what was coming? *Dear God,* Michael thought, *the thongs of whose sandals…*

"Sometimes I can't bear to look at that picture," Tessa said. She brushed tears from her eyes. "But in heaven, surely Jesus comes...."

Michael hugged her with an arm around her shoulders. "He has no regrets, I'm sure."

True to her experience, most of the second album, ministry, had photographs of the church in Asia: Cambodian refugee women wrapping spring rolls for camp construction workers; a Catholic sister in Thailand holding in her arms a child desperately ill from AIDS; a resident of Hong Kong teaching a Sunday school class on the roof of a high-rise apartment building; a Korean missionary family being seen off by friends at the airport; a male student sweeping the walkway of a seminary in Taiwan.

"You'll have to expand your travels," Michael said.

"The project's nowhere near finished. A few from Africa— though not enough, some from Central America, hardly any from Europe or South America. And you probably know, I rarely take assignments in the States."

"There'll be time." Michael closed the album and set it aside. "Now for the eleven treasures." Seeing her expression, he gave her another brief hug. "Don't look so worried. When you said you were furthering God's cause in the world, I had no idea this is what you meant. They're great."

She gave a brief smile, clearly not yet at ease.

He understood her anxiety even less after opening the final album. The first picture showed a park in Japan on a gloomy, overcast day. A young man sat on a park bench, an open Bible on his lap, watching a second, older man rising from the bench, his hand thrown backwards in a gesture of dismissal. Such desperate regret and disappointment permeated the younger man's face, Michael decided the older man must be his father—a disappointment communicated even more poignantly

213

because of the clouds, the gray light, and the weeping willow in the background.

"I saw these two men one day talking in the park close to my mother's apartment," Tessa explained. "I took a picture; it was okay. I took another the next day; still nothing remarkable. I had the feeling they had a standing appointment during the younger man's lunch break. The third day I went back, just to see if they'd be there again, and came away with this picture. I went up to the young man afterwards—you see his name in the caption. The older man is the uncle who raised him. Out of a genuine affection, he agreed to let the young man make his case for Christianity. But you see the result."

"And was that the end?" Michael said.

"I sent him copies of the three pictures with both a promise to pray and a request that he let me know at my father's address if his uncle ever believed." Tessa shook her head. "No response yet."

Michael turned to the next photograph, and then the next, understanding more and more why she called each a miracle. Halfway through he pressed a kiss against her hair, too moved to speak. This picture showed a Vietnamese man, perhaps thirty or thirty-five, being shouted down by someone in the military. Even as the officer screamed into his face, mere inches away, the Vietnamese Christian was holding out a small book to him: the Gospel of John, the caption said, which he had been handing out to passersby.

"I was with a tour group," Tessa said. "Our guide took us down a wrong street. We had to double back, and in the process we stumbled across this confrontation. With so many to keep track of, the poor guide became flustered, and I managed not only to get the shot off but unload the film and hide it in my bra before he hustled us away." She laughed. "I was afraid they would confiscate our film. They didn't."

Michael kept turning the pages, lingering over each picture. In the last, an Indian woman was walking with her child past a crowded temple, oblivious to the noisy celebration around her. A gleam of light caught the gold cross around her neck, providing a fiery focal point to the picture. He ran his hand slowly over the image.

Tessa was gripping the front of her dress. "I was gawking at the parade, of course, something she wouldn't let herself do, when I happened to see her coming down the road. She looked very stiff and remote, and I didn't understand why at first, and then somehow it came to me that she disapproved of what was going on, and I knew I had to get her picture. I jumped up onto the van I had been riding in, managed to duck down on the roof long enough so she wouldn't notice me, fixed my focal length, and took the picture that you see. Honestly, I didn't even know about the cross around her neck. That was God, all God."

He touched the blazing cross again, amazed at the power of the visual image, then closed the book and took her hand in his, "I'll give you the highest compliment I know, Tessa: these pictures will be shown in heaven."

She laughed a little shakily. "You're sweet, Michael, but what are you thinking? Rembrandt on this wall, Caravaggio on the next, and over here Tessa Brooks?"

"Don't joke. Li Hua is right, you know: We're all on assignment here to make him happy, and what you've caught in these albums does exactly that."

"You think so?" She sucked in a breath, clearly distressed.

"I'm sure of it."

"Then..."

Incredibly she looked ready to cry. He didn't understand it.

How could his praise cause so much pain?

"Thank you," she finally said. "I've often wondered—" She stopped herself. "But if you approve…"

"I do approve," he said, hoping to reassure. "It's a wonderful collection. I can't wait to see it finished."

She shook her head more vehemently, and the strands of hair behind her ear fell forward, hiding her face. *What on earth?*

He waited, but she remained silent. "Do you mind if I look through them again?" he finally said.

"Help yourself." She excused herself to get something to drink.

Jillian returned soon after, and Michael suggested supper, but Tessa begged an early night—Mumbai tomorrow.

At his own apartment, he went out onto the balcony and stood against the railing. By stretching just a little he could see the corner of her window, fourth floor up, third one over. What had she meant by "I've often wondered"? And why had his approval made her so sad? It didn't make any sense.

He waited until her light went off, then sat wearily back onto a patio chair. A week in India, two in Australia, and then she'd be leaving. Hope was running out. It seemed all he had left was prayer.

The thought made him smile.

It might be his last hope. It was still his best.

SIXTEEN

Tessa slept through most of the long flight to Mumbai. Arriving late Monday afternoon, she was impressed immediately by the contrast between Mumbai and Singapore. She had always found much to enjoy in India, especially outside the big cities; the long, open views, the bullock-slow pace, the variety and beauty and expression in the people's faces. This time, even the city delighted her. Michael was right again. For all the filth and smell and poverty around her, there was something extra as well, something Singapore was missing. She had the sensation, standing on a busy Mumbai street corner, of being in the midst of a crowded playground during recess with all the crazy, liberated energy exploding around her.

She took her slate of photographs in the executive offices of TransIndus Corporation on Tuesday and was supposed to fit in a shoot at the factory located on the outskirts of Mumbai late that afternoon. Because of an unexpected shutdown, that session was postponed until Thursday, however, pushing back her return to Singapore until Friday. She called Ivy with apologies.

"Oh, don't worry," Ivy said, more graciously than she needed to. "We'll start in the afternoon. Can you make it by one, maybe two? We'll work into the evening if necessary."

Tessa also called the photography shop where she had arranged to have some of her camera equipment cleaned on Friday and after a little begging received permission to bring the equipment by later in the day.

Counting herself fortunate, Tessa traveled uneventfully early Wednesday to a region northwest of Mumbai to photograph two factories clustered there, and finished the final factory, located on the outskirts of Mumbai, on Thursday. Taking the red-eye late Thursday night, she made it back to Singapore on Friday morning.

It hadn't been the smartest idea to squeeze the Mumbai shoot between the Soons and Australia, at least not considering her schedule. She would barely have time to sit down before her plane left again. Leaving her equipment at the photo shop, she arranged to pick it up later that evening, managed a quick shower at the apartment, and arrived after one at Ivy's office.

"Hey, girl, there you are," she said. "You look beat."

"I am," Tessa admitted, "but I've been looking forward to this all week. How'd the pictures turn out?"

"Wonderful, which gives us the welcome difficulty of narrowing our choices down. We've got the projector set up down the hall. Can I have Ellie bring you something?"

"Tea would be great, thank you, and some ice water."

Ivy paused. "You did eat? No, I can see you haven't. Ellie, order up some sandwiches and cake, and bring them down with some tea—hot? with cream and sugar? What am I saying—you've been in India! Of course you want cream and sugar."

Tessa couldn't help but laugh. "I can see things are going well with the project. You're in a very good mood."

"Things are going superbly. Hey, you got to liking the Soons, didn't you?"

"How did you choose them anyway?"

"One of Soon Khim's superiors at the television station is on the advisory board for the book. When we mentioned highlighting a multigenerational family, Soon Khim's name came up." She pushed a conference door open. "Ah, here's the rest of the team. Where's Danny?"

"Had to go home sick," one of the other women said.

"That's right. Too bad." Ivy indicated an empty chair across from the camera projector. "Have a seat and let me explain procedures. We'll have a book with around three hundred thirty pages. Counting titles and index and credits and so forth, that leaves us about thirty pages per family. We're thinking between twenty to forty pictures, though it will probably be on the shorter end, since we want some nice large layouts. Still with me?"

Tessa nodded. Most of the people in the room were young, close enough to Ivy's age, but for all their cheerfulness and energy, Ivy was clearly in charge.

"We've looked through all your transparencies and narrowed them down to a tray. What we want from you is whether there are any in this group of eighty that you absolutely despise, and perhaps ten you'd like to see published. You know these people after all. You can give us a lot of insight into which pictures reveal their family life best. All set? Okay, then, lights, projector! Let's get going."

Whoever had filled the tray had done so chronologically, giving Tessa the pleasant sensation of living through the week with the Soons again. As the projection continued, she kept her own tally of funny, poignant, active; outside, inside; bright and overcast; food and food preparation; and both the number of times each family member was represented and the number of group shots.

The picture of Soon Khim holding a sleeping Ah Kheng in front of the television made the cut, as did the one with Ah Mooi making a pouty face about Long John Silver's. But Tessa's crashing jolt on the playground had been wasted, and the pictures at Mei Ah Koh's high school were less than inspired.

"I thought you may be anxious with those," Ivy's assistant said. She loaded a partially filled second tray. "Here are some others of Mei Koh."

Tessa chose a replacement with a more interesting composition and a better background selection of students. Other than that, after going through the tray numerous times, she approved the other photographs, marking fourteen that she particularly liked.

"Okay, that's it for today," Ivy announced after six o'clock. "Have a good evening, everyone, and I'll see you tomorrow bright and early. We're going to keep pressing on until this project is finished."

She walked Tessa to the elevator. "We'll be keeping many of your photos on file, so let us know if we can help you with them in any way. I wish I could come out for some dinner with you, but I'll be here late tonight."

"No problem," Tessa said. She held out her hand. "Thank you, Ivy. This has been a memorable assignment for a number of reasons, one of them getting to know you."

"Hey, look me up if you're ever back in Singapore." She leaned closer so that the other employees gathered around the elevator doors couldn't hear her. "And if I spot another job you could help us with, you'll be hearing from me—count on it."

"Actually," Tessa said, thinking of the doors at the Soons' Housing and Development Board units, "I might call you myself with some ideas."

Ivy nodded. "Until then."

After picking up her cameras at the shop, Tessa had the taxi pull up close to the western end of Orchard Road so that she could buy some laundry soap. The delay in India had thrown her schedule off. She had managed to finish her correspondence at the airport the night before, including a response to Michael's e-mail asking her if they could meet at the airport for breakfast the next day. He'd be flying in from a hastily arranged trip to the States; she'd be on her way out to Australia. What did she think? She had accepted but wished now that she hadn't. She still had clothes to wash and pack before morning and supplies to check before she could sleep. Breakfast with Michael was one more thing to worry about.

When Tessa passed a display of custard apples, perfectly formed and ever so slightly squashy, in the small grocery store, she couldn't resist. If she couldn't enjoy a stress-free evening, she could at least eat. From the grocery, she went next door to a deli to complete the purchases for one of her favorite snacks: a loaf of French bread, some fresh creamery butter, and a bar of dark, rich chocolate.

She finished everything, including a rescue trim on her hair and a quick e-mail to her mother, by 10:30. Now for her few moments of indulgence....

She put some mellow jazz on Jillian's CD player, set the French bread on the coffee table, flanked by the butter and dark chocolate, and broke the custard apple open. Surely one of the most decadent fruits imaginable, the custard apple had quickly become a favorite Asian treat for Tessa. Properly ripe, its dark green outer covering broke open easily, revealing sunflower-sized seeds, each wrapped with deliciously sweet, creamy-colored pulp. But she wouldn't eat any yet. First a piece of bread, slathered with butter and topped with a chunk of dark chocolate, then the custard apple. Incredible! The perfect balance of flavors.

She was lying back on the sofa, one arm draped behind her head, the other dragging on the floor beside her, when Jillian walked in an hour later. Tessa turned her head toward the door and waved, too relaxed even to laugh at Jillian's surprised expression.

"This is therapy," she explained and waved at the remains of her snack. "Want some chocolate?"

Jillian came a little closer. "You're not drunk, are you?"

This time Tessa had to laugh. "No, though I've always thought champagne would be the perfect addition to my little feast." She pulled herself to sitting position and stretched her arms out as far as they would go. "Sit down," she said, "and try this: fresh French bread—it has to be absolutely fresh—topped with the best quality butter and a chunk of chocolate—highest possible fat content, of course. Take a big bite and add a chaser of custard apple—oh, I'm sorry. I ate both of them."

"It's okay," Jillian said. She sat down in the armchair beside the couch and stared at the remains. "I'll pass, thanks."

Tessa grinned and flopped back full-length onto the couch again.

"Bombay must have been a real trip," Jillian said.

"Nothing disastrous. Just a little delay."

It wasn't India that was stressing her out. It was decisions and questions and regrets and confusion. She didn't want to care anymore. She'd just enjoy what life offered and then move on. Why not? It had always worked before.

"How about you?" she asked Jillian. "Good week?"

No answer came. Through half-opened eyes, Tessa saw Jillian still watching her.

"What is it?" Tessa propped herself up on an elbow.

"I've been thinking about you."

"Have you?"

Jillian's eyes became even more cautious. "I assumed last

weekend that Michael had told you what happened to me. He didn't, did he?"

"No. Should he have?"

Jillian shrugged. "Who expects integrity these days? Though I suppose with Michael I should have. I just thought it would be impossible for him to keep this story to himself."

"I see."

Jillian laughed. "The funny thing is, now that I know he didn't tell you, I'm not sure I want to either...you know. Let's just say I had a scary experience and leave it at that."

"Okay. If that's how you want it." Tessa laid back down and looped an arm over her face, shielding her eyes. It was past time for her to be in bed. If she didn't move soon, she'd fall asleep right here on the couch.

"I do have a question, though," Jillian said.

"Oh?"

"If you wanted to thank your God for something good he did—or something bad he didn't do—how would you do it?"

"God?" Tessa rubbed her eyes, chasing away drowsiness, and sat up properly. "You *want* to do this—thank God?"

"Why not?"

"Well..." Tessa swallowed, unsure how to proceed. *Help!* "You can say thank you, but that's not enough, you know. It's *you* he wants, an ongoing relationship, your devotion and love and obedience. Nothing less will do."

Jillian stared back at Tessa, her face revealing nothing.

"Jillian, it's what we were made for—that relationship with him. You must have sensed him working in your life. Perhaps that's where this impulse to thank him comes from."

Jillian stood. "It was just an idea. Good night."

Tessa flopped back down on the couch. *It's what you want*

from me, too, isn't it? I hope so, 'cause you've got me. I hope it's enough.

"You're weighted down," Michael said when he saw Tessa enter the airport the next morning. "Do you want to check in first?"

"I can stay on this side of the passport control booths, can't I, even if do check in?"

"Of course. Give me your duffel bag."

In line, he asked about her photo conference.

"It was great, thank you."

She obviously didn't want to elaborate. He let the subject drop, and silence fell with it.

"Ready for some breakfast?" he said after check-in. "There's a coffee shop upstairs."

"Sure."

They went through a cafeteria line to get their food, then sat at tables overlooking the waiting area beneath. She asked about New York, he asked about India, but she wasn't really listening. He doubted she would remember anything that was said.

It would be like this every time she left, he realized. She'd be already thinking about that other life waiting at the end of her flight, already there in spirit, her anxieties directed there, her efforts and energy. Would she have enough left over for him at the end? Would her life with him ever matter as much?

A call for her flight finally came.

At her gate, he held her back. "I have something for you. Don't worry, you have time." He pulled a cap from his carry-on bag, a black cap like her White Sox one, except with a brilliantly colored butterfly on the front. "I saw this in the States and thought of you." He held it out. "Please take it."

People pushed past her. Someone nearby spoke. She barely noticed.

She traced the butterfly wings, open and ready for flight, and he saw an ineffable sadness cloud her eyes. "I suppose you're right," she said. "It is long past time for this butterfly to go."

"Tessa!"

She pulled her own cap from the pocket of her Eastpak and held it out to him. "Find a trash can on your way out. I'd rather have yours." After a brief hesitation, she reached up and kissed his cheek. "Good-bye, Michael."

"Wait!"

But she was already moving away, out of reach, toward her flight.

He released a pent-up breath. Another departure.

SEVENTEEN

As always on assignment, the hours in Australia rushed by, and with each successful picture, Tessa welcomed a renewed sense of satisfaction. This was what she lived for, this feeling. This was what she could give to life, this skill, this passion. She was fortunate to be doing something she loved so much. She told herself this constantly.

And yet, late at night, muscles too sore for easy sleep, she found her thoughts slipping inevitably toward Michael. Finally, on Thursday night, imagining him on the soccer field with the children clustered around him, she began praying for him; for his soccer, first, and then his Bible class; his work and his health and his safety. And in that moment of vulnerability, before a God she knew loved her, the tears finally came.

She wanted to be with him, to see him smile and share the moments of his life. Wanted it even in the midst of a dream assignment, one any photographer would covet.

In the sky above the balcony outside, a slivered moon shone in a cloudless sky, reflecting the tightness in her heart. She sat in the corner, pressed her cheek against the rail, and wished for another balcony, his voice on the phone, and easy friendship.

Four years ago when romance beckoned, she had enjoyed the experience, but when he broke off their relationship, she had said good-bye with little hesitation and only mild disappointment. She hadn't needed him, not then. She'd been complete without him, and he must have known it. No wonder he had never pursued anything further.

She hugged her arms around her legs.

No mild disappointment this time. It scared her, how much she already missed him, and yet what choice did she have? Even Michael saw the value of her photography now. He had proved that with each word of praise he gave her church pictures. He had even agreed the work should go on.

So what now? Wanting Michael, not having him; unable to give up her career, unable to completely enjoy it. It was an impossible conflict.

She bowed her head and prayed, searching word by word through her storehouse of psalms until she reached the sixteenth, where she finally found some comfort. God was her portion. Not Michael, not photography, but God himself. Maybe that's what he wanted her to learn through all this pain—to put him first. Whether the boundary lines of her life would fall in pleasant places, she couldn't know, but this thing she did know: she would always have God on her side.

That should be enough.

Back in Singapore on Sunday, a week and a half later, Tessa stashed her bags in her bedroom at Jillian's apartment and headed toward the kitchen. Empty tomato cans sat on the counters. Spices and flavorings and even the sugar bowl lined the space beside the burners. A pile of lettuce and salad fixings overflowed the colander in one sink. In the other, dirty frying pans and cutting boards, dishes and knives soaked in grimy, soapy water. And in the midst of it all, Jillian was stirring a pot on the stove.

"Hey, you're back," she said, "and in plenty of time. Michael's coming for dinner."

"Oh."

"And can you believe it, I'm trying my mother's recipe for

spaghetti sauce." She held a spoonful of sauce out to Tessa. "It needs to simmer, but what do you think? More salt?"

"Tastes okay."

"Then get yourself something to drink and sit down, because I have something to tell you."

"About Michael?"

Jillian thought this was funny. "Poor confused Tessa. You've been all wrong about us, you know. He's one of the best friends I have, but that's all." She gave a rueful smile. "I've always known it wouldn't go any further, not with Michael." She grinned at Tessa's reaction, then turned to stir the sauce one more time before sitting down across from Tessa. "No, what's been going on in my life has nothing to do with that. Just the opposite. The truth is, these last few weeks I thought I might be HIV-positive."

Tessa blinked. "HIV? You mean—AIDS?"

"That Friday at Harry's—I was drunk, and Michael took me out, remember? I'd gotten a call the day before from a guy I dated a couple of years ago who tested positive and thought I should know." She swore. "That's a laugh. I should have known a long time ago, but no one ever thinks it's going to happen to them, do they?"

"That's awful."

Jillian tipped her beer bottle, watched the liquid run close to overflowing, then back down again. "I didn't tell anyone, only Michael. It was too weird. I don't know what I would have done without him. He suggested I fly up to Hong Kong to be tested, got the tickets for me, made all the arrangements. Singapore's too small, he said. Someone would hear. I'm sure he was right."

"But you only *thought* you might test positive. You didn't?"

"Waiting was the pits, and then when I could have called, I

chickened out. Michael did it for me. That last day you were on assignment, remember? That's when he found out, after he got back from the zoo. We ate at the Compass Rose to celebrate." She looked at Tessa a little more closely. "I thought you should know, because afterwards, I don't know, you looked a little doubtful. About Michael, I mean."

Tessa shook her head, still not clear. "But the test was negative?"

"Well, for sure up to twelve weeks before I took it. After that—" Jillian shook her head. "Who can tell?"

Tessa winced.

"I know," Jillian said. "You're thinking about Hugo, aren't you? I'm not in the clear yet, not if he's infected. But there is this—at least I can stop worrying about the men I've slept with since Alex." She hugged her arms across her chest. "How could I have lived that down, if I'd passed it on to someone else? How could anyone get over that? You know, more than anything, that's what got me thinking about God—living it down, I mean."

"Oh, Jillian." Tessa gripped Jillian's hand. So much pain and worry, and through it all she'd been oblivious. Then Jillian's words registered. "Are you saying…do you mean with God? Jillian, you can't live *anything* down with God."

"What do you mean?"

"I'm not sure you want to hear this."

"Yes, I do. Go ahead."

"Okay. It's like you have a can of perfectly, absolutely, completely white paint. Drop red paint into the can, even just one little smidgen, and it's not white anymore. That's what sin does to us, even the smallest sin. God insists on perfect purity. It doesn't matter how much you try, you can't make things right again, whether your sin is infecting a person with AIDS or bringing a pencil home from work."

Jillian stared back at her. "That hardly seems fair."

"It certainly explains the appeal of religions like Buddhism and Hinduism. In those, do a small sin, work it off. Do a big sin, it takes a little longer. Either way, you have complete control of your fate."

"So? Why not? What's the matter with that?"

"For me? Because the god in those religions is basically impersonal. He might provide an occasional educational opportunity—the Buddha telling people how to live or Krishna coming down to exemplify godliness. He might occasionally grant you a favor, with the understanding, of course, that you'll pay up eventually. But mostly he's a scorekeeper. If you never reach nirvana, he doesn't care. There's no affection, no forgiveness, no friendship with that god. You don't matter to him."

"And your God's different?"

"Yes! We matter a lot to him. He feels with us, the Bible says, weeps over us, draws us like chicks under his wings. He sings over us with joy and plans for us and walks so close beside us that he keeps us in his shadow. And one day, when we see him, he will speak to us face to face, as a man speaks to his friend. That's what God offers, you know. It's different than other religions—he gives himself."

"On the understanding I sign myself over to him first, of course. I know how it works. What a deal."

Tessa shook her head. "It's not like that, Jillian, not with God."

Jillian grunted. "He has expectations. And if I mess up—well, we've talked about this before."

"Listen, Jillian. Hindus, Muslims, Buddhists—they're constantly negotiating, it's true. All these acts of devotion you see around here, these rituals people take part in, they do them to gain their gods' approval, to coerce some blessing from them or do penance for some wrongdoing. But I don't have to wheedle blessings out of God. He promises those freely, out of love. And I don't have to work off my sins, either, whatever you're thinking. They've all been forgiven—past and present. That's what Jesus accomplished on the cross. I obey him because I want to. No more bartering. No manipulation. Just the freedom of loving and being loved."

"That sounds pretty strange," Jillian said.

"It shouldn't. What you've done with your sister and brother, paying their bills, taking care of them—no one's making you do that. Isn't that an example of the love I'm talking about? You may not have received much of that kind of love, but you've certainly been giving it."

"Not perfectly."

Tessa smiled, dipping her head in concession. "Who does, except God?"

Jillian got up to stir the meat, then leaned back against the counter. "I did go to confession last week and to mass on Sunday. That's what I grew up in, you know—the Catholic church, at least until my father cut out on us."

"How'd it go?"

"Different than Michael's church, that's for sure. People at his church seemed to be gearing up for a party or something, moving around before the service, laughing and talking about anything that came to mind. This was better—everyone quiet, and people going up so solemnly and bowing to take communion, and the priest dressed in his robes, and the prayers thought out ahead of time so they were just right. It made it all seem more real to me—like God might actually be there." She twirled the pot holder once all the way around on her finger, then rocked it gently, back and forth. "I liked the liturgy, too. It calmed my heart. 'Lord, have mercy. Christ, have mercy. Lord, have mercy.'"

The pot holder stopped swaying, just hung from her finger, suspended for a long moment. Then, with a weary breath, Jillian let her arms sag. "I wish I could believe what you say about God. It seems too easy somehow. And yet the possibility of starting over again with a real chance of pleasing him—" She paused and rubbed her eyes.

The sauce bubbled behind her. She turned the fire down and found a lid.

"Will you go back again?" Tessa said. "To mass?"

"I think so. Maybe. Anyway—" She began gathering the empty cans. "Enough of that. Michael will be here soon, and I should go get some French bread, don't you think?"

Tessa stumbled up. "When's he coming?"

"Not right away. Six or six-thirty." Jillian grinned, amused all over again. "Don't worry. You have time to get ready."

Jillian sent Tessa to the door when Michael knocked. He was frowning when she opened it, but promptly cleared his face. "So you made it back."

"Of course I did." She felt his scrutiny and pulled the door wider. "Come in, please. Jillian has instructed me to entertain you in the living room while she finishes the salad."

She waited until he took the seat opposite the couch, then gave him her brightest smile. "I've had some great news."

"Have you?"

"I talked to my agent on Friday. He thinks he might have a job lined up for me in Turkey, three weeks, an in-depth feature. I'm really excited. Did you know there are only about twelve hundred Christians in Turkey, out of 63 million people?"

"When does the assignment start?"

"In three or four months. Ray's still working out the details. And he's thinking perhaps an essay on orphanages in China and maybe even a *National Geographic* assignment in Karachi, Pakistan—one of their city features. That would be pretty exciting. It's hard to get in with that magazine."

"Is it?" Michael began cleaning his glasses. His eyes seemed softer, somehow, or was it just that he looked very, very tired?

"You look exhausted, Michael. Have you had a hard couple of weeks?"

"My own fault. No problem." He replaced his glasses and went on conversationally. "From the one e-mail you sent, you didn't have too easy a time, either."

"I'd have been smarter to choose one pregnant teenager, as I had originally planned, but that would have meant failing to show the scope of these people's medical needs, and I wanted to do that. If only they had more qualified personnel!"

"No doubt."

"Oh, don't say it," she said, finding a laugh. "Countless places have even less health care available. But I wasn't in *those* places, Michael. It wasn't those doctors and nurses I saw working so hard."

"Your pictures are sure to help. But you never said—did you get anything for your worldwide church?"

"No. I was too rushed. I squeezed church in, just because I was so curious, but otherwise I was on the move the entire time."

"And now you'll have a break."

"Yes."

After a pause she brought up her next assignment, a feature on Lake Toba in Sumatra, scheduled for shoot in three weeks. They managed to stay on that topic until Jillian called them to the dining room table and, once seated, Jillian was on hand to help the conversation along. Even so, Tessa felt on edge. That Sunday, eating chili crab at Ponggol, she and Michael had carried the spoken conversation, with Jillian the real focus of Michael's attention. Now she had taken Jillian's role. She felt his attention on her, knew she was doing a very poor job of pretending nonchalance, and yet what did he expect from her?

As soon as possible, she stood. "I'll clear out these dishes now if everyone's done."

She kept her eyes on what she was collecting and then pushed her way through the swinging door.

Jillian followed her in and took a bakery box with three cannoli from the refrigerator. "You all right?" she asked Tessa as she began transferring them to a plate.

"Fine. A little tired, but okay."

Jillian stopped. "Then how come you're in here watching me serve this and not out there with him?"

Tessa winced. "Well…"

Jillian chuckled. "Bring that last plate when you come, will you?" And she disappeared through the swinging door.

After dessert, Jillian announced she was meeting her friend Rosey and some men from her office. "If you don't want to do the dishes, just pile them in the sink. I'll get to them."

And then she disappeared, leaving Tessa with Michael.

Tessa gulped down such a large bite of the Italian delicacy that she had trouble keeping her mouth closed while she chewed.

Michael sat back and watched her try, which she thought was rude of him. She would have told him so, too, if he hadn't first handed her a glass of water. He waited while she wiped her mouth, and then folded her hand into his.

"Now tell me what's wrong," he said. "You're worried about something."

"Me, worried? No!" She freed her hand to wave off his concern. "If I look anxious, it's because I only have the one short assignment lined up for the next few months. I'll feel better after I talk with my agent. I'm sure he can find something else for me."

"You're afraid you won't have enough work? That's why you're on edge?" He shook his head. "I don't believe you."

"It's true." She scraped a bit of whipped cream onto her spoon and stuffed it into a suddenly dry mouth. "I'm always this way at the end of an assignment."

"Tessa." His voice was low and determined. "This has nothing to do with work."

"It does! I've been here too long, that's all. I'll feel better once I've left Singapore." She stood and began collecting the dishes. "Anyway, I'm a little tired. If you don't mind..."

"This is about us, you and me." His hand closed on her arm, and the dishes clattered back onto the table. "I'm the one you're running away from, not Singapore. It's me you want to leave behind."

"No!" She jerked on her arm, but he didn't let go.

"Then prove it. Sit back down and talk to me."

"Why should I?" she demanded. "We're friends again. Why isn't that enough for you?"

"Friends? Is that what you call it?" He stood and, with hands on her shoulders, turned her toward him. Blue eyes challenged hers. "Friends trust each other, Tessa, and the truth is, except for showing me your pictures, which I pushed you into doing, you've never once told me what's on your heart, your plans or fears or dreams—and you've certainly never asked me." He paused, fighting for control. "We *have* to talk, Tessa. There are barriers between us we can't get around any other way."

"Then why bother?" She hugged her arms tightly across her chest. "Let's just go on from here, make the most of what we have."

He shook his head, the grip on her arms tightening. "But the 'most' of what we have isn't very much, is it? And going on from here means going in different directions. I think you know that, Tessa."

He waited, the pallor on his face very apparent. She remained silent.

"I see," he said. "That's what you want." He released her and stepped back. "Then so be it. Have a good trip, Tessa—wherever it is you're going."

She tried to sleep after he left, tried a shower, more food, even did the dishes. Still too keyed up to relax, Tessa finally yanked the package from the end of her bed and unloaded the year-books and pictures. Jenny had gone to the trouble of sending them. She might as well take a look. Sitting on her bed, she worked her way through the one college yearbook she had from her freshman year, then leafed through all four high school books.

Nothing.

She set these aside and lifted a flat box filled with pictures from Jenny's package. Incredibly, there near the top, she found a picture of a twenty-two-year-old Michael, standing beside her in front of the big Buddha at Kamakura in Japan. Had her hair really been that long? Michael looked so thin, almost gangly, but with the same careful intelligence, the same barely visible humor. How unfair that men only improved with age!

She fell asleep holding the photograph and woke to find her cheek pressed against it on the pillow. Pale sunshine filtered in through the window, lighting the yearbooks still spread across her bed. She dragged herself up and went looking for coffee.

"I'm just making it," Jillian said, already dressed for work. "I'll bring you a cup."

Tessa gratefully climbed back into bed and pushed up her pillows behind her. With the photograph of Michael safely tucked into her Bible, she propped Blake's picture against her alarm clock to have it handy for comparison purposes and pulled the yearbooks closer.

Setting Tessa's coffee down on the bedside table, Jillian couldn't help but see the picture. "Blake again? You're not secretly attracted to him are you? Because if you are—"

"No," Tessa said. "Trust me. I've been trying to figure out where I've seen him before, that's all."

"He can't remember you?"

"No. I asked, but—" She shook her head. "Nothing."

"Must be hard making the connection, when you meet so many people in your work."

"Which is why, if I can't see anything in these yearbooks and old photos, I'm going to drop it and get out of here. Don't be surprised if I pack up and leave today."

"You're kidding. Today?" Her eyes narrowed. "Does Michael know?"

"I think he has a pretty good idea. Don't worry. I'll call at the bank before I go."

"Just like that, huh? What a life. You know—" Jillian pushed a yearbook over to make room for herself on the bed. "You can stay free this week, if you want—if that's what's rushing you out of here."

"Thanks, but I've got lots of reasons to go."

"And most of them have to do with Michael, don't they?"

Tessa shrugged. "It's an old story."

"Yeah, I finally figured that out, more from the way Michael's been acting than you. He's been pretty miserable these last two weeks."

Tessa pressed her lips together. A horrible, huge, bulgy ache was developing in her stomach, and she swallowed hard to push it down before shaking her head.

"Then, here," Jillian said, "I better give you a hug while I can. Take care of yourself, Tessa Brooks, and stay in touch."

Left alone, Tessa slumped down into her pillows. Definitely time to go, the sooner the better. She thought of Jillian's last words and winced. *Stay in touch?* If her inability to recognize Blake was anything to judge by, most of the people she met didn't even stay in her memory.

With a sigh Tessa picked up a yearbook again. Page by page, she found nothing, and the loose collection of photos seemed equally improbable. Then, halfway through the stack, reaching for a picture of her roommate Nikki, Tessa saw him.

Finally.

He was in the background, but in clear focus and well-lit. She remembered him now. Nikki had dated him near the beginning of their second semester. His face was younger and thinner in the picture, and he had lighter brown hair, but he was definitely Blake.

It was the name that had changed.

The student Tessa had known in college was called Tim Heslop.

And no wonder she had been nervous.

Back in college, in spite of an easy, attractive charm, he had turned both Tessa and Nikki off: too willing to hand in a plagiarized paper, too quick to badmouth an acquaintance, too glib in shirking the blame for wrecking his parents' car. On his third date with Nikki, he'd forged his mother's signature on a check, and even bragged about it. That was enough for Nikki. She dumped him. It was only afterward that she discovered her credit cards were missing....

Tessa slumped further back into her pillow.

Whatever the reason for his assumed identity now, it didn't bode well for the bank—or for Michael. Wasn't Blake his responsibility?

Groping herself into shorts and a T-shirt, she shoved the two pictures of Blake, college and contemporary, into her back pocket, and picked up the phone. The receptionist at the bank connected her to Jillian.

"Tessa! I'm sorry, Michael's not here. Did you find someone who looked like Blake in those yearbooks?"

Tessa gave a little squeak. "He can't hear you, can he?"

"What? No...I doubt it." But her voice had dropped notice-ably. "Sorry. I didn't realize it was a secret. You did say you had talked to him. Now he's gone somewhere. It's okay. Anyway, Michael's in a meeting. I'll tell him to call."

"As soon as possible."

"I can interrupt him if you want."

"Just ask him to call," Tessa said. "I'll wait."

She made herself some breakfast, vacuumed the dining room, cleaned the bathroom, and began her packing. Finally, a little before ten, she plopped down on the end of the couch and stared at the phone. If Michael didn't call in the next fifteen minutes, she was going down to the bank herself.

To her great relief, she heard a knock on the door.

EIGHTEEN

M ichael," Tessa said and threw the door open. "It's about—oh."

"Hello, Tessa." Blake planted a hand on the door and pushed, shoving Tessa backwards, and leaving himself space to enter. He shut the door behind him, then crossed his arms and sneered at Tessa. "You didn't expect me, did you? I'm glad to see you're dressed. Get your purse and let's go."

She took another step backwards. "Where?"

"Don't play stupid with me. If you've been looking for me in your college yearbooks, you already know too much." His eyes hardened. "You do know, don't you, who I am?"

She tried to turn, intent on putting as much distance between them as possible, but he grabbed her arm and gave a hard shake. "Answer my question. You know who I am, don't you?"

"What happened to your southern accent?"

He moved his face even closer, so that his breath washed over her. "Go on. Say my name."

She turned her face in distaste. "Tim Heslop."

"And that about says it all. I can hear it in your voice. Well, forget getting in touch with Michael." He released her with a shove, causing her to stumble back. "Get your stuff. You're coming with me."

"Why should I?"

"Because, honey, I've got a gun in my coat pocket, which I won't hesitate to use." He pulled it out. It fit neatly into the palm of his hand.

"A gun? You carry a gun around with you? In Singapore?"

"Just shut up and do what I say." He pushed it into her side. "I want you to get your passport and whatever other documents you need to travel."

"Wait! Travel?" She tried to pull away. "I'm not going anywhere, not with you."

The gun jammed harder against her ribs. "Do what I say."

"Okay, okay. They're in my bedroom."

She had forgotten the yearbooks and photos scattered on her bed.

Blake stiffened when he saw them. "So here they are. Show me the yearbook."

"I didn't—It was Nikki. Her picture made me remember. You weren't in any of the yearbooks, really."

"Still, I wonder…"

He didn't move. Her heart was thumping, and she felt perspiration on her palms and neck. A giggle threatened—not a yearbook, just two pictures jammed into her back pocket. Would he see them?

Please God, let me keep a grip here. Be my help, please.

He shrugged and twisted the gun harder against her ribs. "Who cares? Even with a picture, people won't find me. I know how to disappear—the great advantage of having a face no one notices. Now, where is that passport?"

He seemed pleased, for some reason, that she kept her important papers in a belly pack, but insisted she bring along her Eastpak as well—"Minus the cameras, of course." He tucked the belly pack inside the backpack, hefted it over his own shoulder, and pushed her toward the door.

"Wait," Tessa said. "If I'm traveling, won't I need more than this?"

"Just come. We'll walk to my apartment from here. I'm two units down from Michael's. Until we get there, not another

241

word." He glanced into the hallway, then pushed her against the wall inside the apartment a moment longer. "I'm putting the gun into my pocket, but it will be easy to reach, and I won't think twice about shooting you and the person you appeal to. Got that?"

Tessa nodded.

"Then let's go," Blake said. "Nice and easy."

He prodded her down the hall and toward the elevator. "Breathe," he said. "I can't have you fainting on me."

Outside, they passed groundskeepers, a Caucasian woman with two small children, and a Filipino maid carrying groceries. Blake greeted each politely, his words smooth, his smile friendly. But his grip on Tessa's arm felt like a steel band, and his right hand, she noticed, remained in his pocket, holding the gun.

"Smart girl," he said as he shut his apartment door behind him. He pushed her into the kitchen. "Right there—bottom drawer. Open that up. Good. See that rope? Bring it."

In the dining area, he tied Tessa to a chair, then disappeared into his bedroom. Alone for the moment, Tessa looked frantically around. There was nothing in view to help her escape. The room, in fact, had no personal touches at all that she could see, no photographs, no flowers, no books on the shelves, not even a magazine on the coffee table.

Of course. No roots. She knew how that worked in her own life. But why would Blake live that way?

He emerged minutes later with an overnight bag and, after a glance her way, sat down at the computer and began working.

Tessa pressed her lips together, appalled to find tears close. She couldn't give in to emotions now. If there was any hope of her getting through this, she needed to think, carefully, rationally.

So think.

He intended to take her with him, that much was clear. Why else would he have insisted she bring her passport? Was he buying himself more time by taking her? Or was he removing her from Singapore so he could kill her anonymously?

Fingers of panic crept up her back.

Please. She couldn't remember how to start Psalm 121, but there was something about coming and going, wasn't there? The Lord will watch over you? That wasn't right, but it was close enough. She said those few words over and over again in her mind—The Lord will watch over you—imagining him close, standing beside her, so close that she was in his shadow, until she was able at last to take a deep, slow breath and relax.

The last option, taking her somewhere so he could kill her, made the most sense of all, but didn't the security at the airport pose a threat? How would he get the gun through the metal detectors?

She tugged on the rope holding her against the chair. If she couldn't get away, she should at least use the time to gain some information from Blake. He was arrogant enough to want to brag, confident enough to think himself safe.

She cleared her throat and offered the bait. "Aren't you even going to explain what's going on?"

He glanced her way. "Can't figure it out, huh? Well, why not tell you? They'll know soon enough, though that won't help them find me, not once I'm finished up here. Thanks to this little warning, there won't be any trace of my accounts for them to follow." He found the files he wanted, plugged a disk into the computer, and spun his chair around to face Tessa. "Blake Hoffman is the name of a real banker from Tennessee who was killed in a small plane crash. It was no big deal to get a copy of his documents: birth certificate, driver's license, social security card, résumé, and diplomas. I took it all to a headhunter in San Francisco, where I said I wanted to work overseas in a bank where I could use my skill making loans."

"But why?"

"What do you think? Since coming here I've made loans of almost two million dollars to nonexistent corporations. It's all in my own accounts, of course." Again he sneered at her. "Bet you never thought old Tim Heslop would do so well."

Two million dollars? For an amount like that, he could easily kill her.

He turned back to his computer. "Just sit there and let me finish what I'm doing. I still have to close out a few accounts, and then we'll be on our way."

He was humming under his breath, and while he waited for something to finish on the computer he tapped his fingers on the table in front of his laptop, the beat light and cheerful. What a rush, for him.

He will keep you from all harm—that's what it was. The Lord will watch over your coming and going, both now and forevermore.

Forever? Was it forever God had planned for her?

Then what about Michael? For the first time, regret and pain broke through the anesthetic effects of panic. She might never talk to him again, not in this life. He would never know—

She tugged on the ropes, scraping them against her wrists. Why wasn't there something nearby, some piece of glass, some other convenient sharp object? She tugged again, the knot hopelessly tight. In a movie, there was always something, why not here? The entire room, in fact, had all the charm of a hotel room, and a cheap one at that. What kind of man lived in such a cold environment?

No wonder he needed such a small suitcase.

The thought disturbed her. Was everything he owned here so cheap—easily left, easily replaced?

He stood, folded the laptop, and put it into his bag. "All right, up." He untied her from the chair, plucked up her backpack and his small bag, and hustled her toward the door. "And the same again—not a word from you in the taxi. I still have the gun." He patted his pocket. "So keep your mouth shut."

In the taxi, his arm tucked around her, he began a conversation with the driver. Tessa didn't listen. She kept thinking about the size of the carry-on bag Blake had insisted on stowing in the taxi's trunk. So much left behind…easily left, easily replaced. What an empty existence.

But was she any different? She also lived a life of quick change and shallow commitment. Always on the outside—taking the picture, framing it, deciding what to include, what to exclude, but never being part of it herself.

She was plenty friendly to people—she had to be. But when had someone last turned to her the way Jillian had turned to Michael? And while she was good at recording the world's problems, from teenage pregnancies among Australian aborigines to religious persecution in Vietnam, when had she last stuck around long enough to do something about them?

A worse thought: Who would care if Blake took her with him now? Who would even notice? She was between assignments, after all, and without professional commitments. Who was counting on her for anything?

Even Michael, after their parting last night, might feel himself well rid of her.

Ah. But she had left her cameras. How stupid of Blake. He should have made her bring them.

She felt sick. People, yes. She would leave them willingly.

Friends, even a fiancé—all of them. But never her cameras.

The taxi was speeding toward the airport, the scenery rushing past her. It seemed to be symbolic of her life. This wasn't what God wanted, this life she led. It wasn't projects or skills or success that pleased him. It was love, love for himself and love for his people.

And whom had she ever really loved?

For all her fine-sounding claims of what she could do for God, she had failed him, and now she might never see Michael again. She yanked her hand free from Blake's and pressed it against her stomach.

"Don't you dare," Blake said.

"What?"

"I don't want you throwing up on me."

"How charming. You probably say that to all your dates."

He twisted her arm. "Shut up. I told you, no talking."

At the airport, after glancing at his watch, he told the driver to go around the circular approach one more time. "I'm sure you understand," he said, laughing, to the driver and pulled Tessa closer. "Much nicer to say good-bye in your taxi."

Tessa suffered his closeness in silence. With his arm around her back, he held her left hand against her shoulder, her arm bent up at the elbow. Her right hand he held in her lap, so tightly she couldn't possibly get away. At least he wasn't kissing her, though he did whisper in her ear—warnings to keep quiet and regrets that he wouldn't be on hand to see the people's reaction at the bank when they discovered his thefts. "Michael, especially, the golden-haired boy who can do no wrong. I'd like to see him trying to live this one down."

"What do you mean?"

"He prides himself so much on guarding against fraud, and all the time the biggest culprit was sitting two desks away."

"At least he doesn't have to cheat to get his money," Tessa hissed.

"No, he just inherited it." He glanced again at his watch and told the driver to stop. "I need my bag, please."

As soon as the driver disappeared from view, Blake grabbed Tessa's backpack, zipped it open, and thrust the gun inside. "Now you have it," he said, "and good luck. Make a scene, call someone over, and you're in big trouble. And just in case you're thinking about following me, forget it. There's security like you wouldn't believe in there—metal detectors are just the beginning—and that gun's black market. Its number's probably on file somewhere. I strongly suggest you just forget about me and head on back to town."

He glanced outside. The driver was waiting with his bag, just outside the taxi door.

"But just in case you get any ideas," he went on, "here's a little added insurance." And he snapped a small lock on the zippered compartment holding the gun. "There. Now you can't dump the backpack and try to follow me, because if you do, you'll be dumping your passport as well."

He leaned closer, so that when he spoke she felt his breath against her neck. "Happy hunting," he whispered, "but you'll never find me."

He climbed out, said something to the driver, and with a quick wave disappeared into the airport.

Relief paramount, she sat in stunned silence for a moment, hands off the offending pack. She had the gun, yes, but neither the freedom nor the heart to use it.

She should at least see where he went. But when she reached for the car handle, the taxi was already moving.

"Wait!" She grabbed the driver's seat. "Where are you going? Let me out."

"No lah. He pay. You in hurry, yes? I take you to Ardmore Park, quick-quick."

"No! You have to stop. Please. Let me out." She saw the driver's surprise, heard her own hysteria, and with a massive effort calmed her voice. "This is his bag," she said, holding the backpack up. "He will want it. Take me back, please. I will pay. No!" She covered her mouth. She couldn't. Her wallet was on the other side of the lock, with the gun and her passport.

"No money." She tried again. "But if you take me back, I will find another taxi. You can keep his money, get another fare, earn more. Please. I must go back. He needs his bag."

It took more of the same to convince him, then longer than she could have guessed to find a place to turn. Traffic during the noon hour was busy, and without the promise of extra money, the driver wasn't in a hurry.

Back at the airport, she went through double glass doors, through another set, and then into the huge waiting area that led toward the ticket booths. The sound struck her first, the way her small footsteps faded into the expanse of air above and around her. How could she hope to spot someone in so vast a place?

And the police, they were everywhere. She clutched the backpack closer, then forced herself to relax. It was hopeless. How could any trained guard not see the guilt on her face?

Swallowing convulsively, she walked forward toward the ticket counter, thinking maybe, by some miracle, he'd had trouble getting through the passport control booths. But she saw no sign of him.

If she'd gotten out of the taxi immediately, she'd have seen him at the ticket counters. No wonder he'd paid for the return fare. He'd even told the driver to hurry.

She sank into a seat in the waiting area. Why do the wicked

prosper? She knew the answer now. Because evil never takes them by surprise.

With a deep breath, she considered her options.

She could find a security office, hand the backpack over, and get their help. If she did it now, they might still be able to catch Blake, that is if they didn't take too long buying her story.

But going to the police might put Michael in an even worse spot. Hadn't he said his bank wouldn't want their problems made public?

So, Michael. She had been resisting the idea of calling him, her sense of independence long engrained and hard to relinquish, but saying his name, knowing she would call, she felt an overwhelming sense of freedom and relief wash over her. He would help her. He would know what to do.

Only this time, please, please, let him be there.

Still without money, she begged a dime off the man at the next telephone booth. When she finally got through to Michael, he heard the desperation in her voice immediately.

"Where are you?" he said. "I called you at Jillian's, but you didn't answer."

"Blake has gone, Michael, he's been stealing. You have to come. I don't know which flight he's taken, and I don't know how to find out."

"Flight? Tessa, what's going on?"

"I'm at the airport. He's gone now, but I'm stranded. Will you come?"

"Stranded?"

"I don't have any money. He brought me—Michael, *please,* just *come.*"

"All right. I will. Tell me where to find you."

"At the phones—no, that's too exposed. I'll be off on the left, as you enter, near that French bakery. Please—hurry."

"It'll be at least forty minutes, maybe longer."

"Just *come*."

Feeling adrift again, she went to stand against the wall near the bakery shop, muscles tight, shoulders hunched, trying somehow to make herself inconspicuous. If Blake, for some bizarre reason, changed his mind and came back for her... She pushed the thought away.

The minutes dragged. Having decided to call him, she found herself longing for his appearance—

She froze. Longing...yes, like watchmen wait for the morning. And she hadn't even thanked him.

She put a hand to her forehead. *How small and absurd we must seem, and you so great and good—unfailing love and full redemption. This time, as always, you have been my salvation, I know it's true, and once again if I stand at all, I stand in your grace, but send Michael soon, please, and thank you, thank you, that he's still willing to come.*

She said Psalm 130 over and over again in her mind as she waited, until gradually she felt herself calming, and then he was there, her own Michael, and though she couldn't remember moving, couldn't remember speaking his name, she did remember afterward the enormous comfort of going into his arms and the sure knowledge of being safe at last.

"Tessa." He folded her close for a long moment, strong arms, a body to hide hers, her face pressed against his shoulder. Then he gripped her arms and held her from him. "What is it?" His eyes searched her face. "Tessa, tell me. What's happened?"

"Blake. He's been stealing from Chadsworth. We should follow him—no, you should go to the police. You might still be able to find out what plane he boarded."

"I'm not going anywhere until you tell me what's going on."

"But there's no time. If you go now, you might still catch him."

"No." Like Blake before him, Michael gripped her arms, but with such a difference. His hands were gentle, their slow movement designed to soothe. "Tessa, I can't help until I know what the problem is."

"Oh, fine, but we're wasting time." She pulled the two photographs of Blake from her back pocket. "Look at these."

"Pictures?"

"Look at them," she said. "Do you see any resemblance?"

"Okay. They're both Blake, obviously. I still don't understand."

"He's *not* Blake Hoffman. That's what I'm trying to tell you. I recognized him. Remember, I said that, a long time ago? And then I was dreaming about him, strange dreams where I was dancing with him but couldn't see his face. And every time I was with him, he avoided me. Not just a cold shoulder; a *frozen* shoulder. I've hardly gotten three clear glimpses of his face all the times I've been near him, much less a good hard look. And I decided it was intentional, that he was avoiding me, and I was right."

"Not Blake Hoffman?"

"His real name is Tim Heslop. He dated my roommate in college. Blake Hoffman is a dead banker from Tennessee. Blake—our Blake—has been using that Blake's name and his birth certificate and résumé and stuff, all to make fake loans—no, not fake loans. Real loans to fake corporations, and keeping the money for himself."

Michael drew back. "At Chadsworth?"

"Two million dollars worth."

He grunted. "You're sure?"

"Michael, there's still time." She motioned toward the security gate. "Go see if you can catch him, or at least figure out which plane he boarded."

"So you were right."

"He explained it all, in his apartment." She leaned close enough to tip her head against his shoulder so she could lower her voice even more. "I would have tried to keep him from leaving, I would have followed him to see what plane he boarded, but he held a gun to me, and then he put it in my backpack, with my passport, and look—he even put a lock on it."

"A gun?" He gripped her arm again, unaware that he was hurting her. His eyes flared with a passionate concern. "He held a gun on you, Tessa?"

"Shhh. It's in my bag."

"What was he thinking?"

"Michael, we could still catch him."

"Stop." He pulled her back against the wall. "Now tell me the whole story, everything that happened. I need to hear it all."

"Okay." As she spoke, his concern grew, and when she got to the gun and thinking why Blake might take her with him, he almost looked sick, his skin was so pale. He lifted her hand and held it against his face. She could feel his jaw clench as she progressed, could see the frustrated anger burning in his eyes, the tension in his cheek.

When she finished, he held her hand to his lips for a long moment, then lifted hooded eyes to hers.

"This is my fault. I should have believed you." He closed his eyes and groaned. "You could have been killed and all because I didn't listen. Tessa—" He kissed her hand again and would have pulled her to him completely, but realized abruptly what he was doing and stopped, stepped back, and released her. "Thank God you're all right. The question is, what now?"

"Shouldn't we try to stop him?"

"No. This has to be Chadsworth's decision." He lifted the backpack. "I'll let them decide." He paused. "Can you come back to the bank with me, tell them what you told me?"

"Of course."

"'Of course.' Listen to you." He gently, very carefully, ran one finger down the line of her hair and tucked it behind her ear. "Such a brave heart, Tessa Brooks. Come on, then. Let's get it over with."

"What about you?" Tessa said in the taxi. "At the bank, I mean. Will they hold you responsible?"

He took her hand again, as he had in the airport, and held it against his cheek.

"He said they'd blame you, Michael. Do you think they will?"

"Tell me the truth, Tessa. Are you really okay? He didn't hurt you?"

"I was afraid," she admitted. "And then when he said you'd have trouble living this down—Michael, I tried, but I couldn't think of any way to stop him. He was so much stronger than I am, and then I was tied up and in the taxi there was the..." She glanced at the driver. "You know. I'm so sorry, Michael."

"Foolish Tessa." He kissed her hand, blue eyes intent upon her. "Don't you know I'd rather give up a hundred careers than have anything happen to you?"

"You would?"

He chuckled low in his throat. "I would."

"Even so—" She gripped his hand. "I hope they don't blame you. That's a lot of money."

"No kidding." He let out a long breath. "Two million dollars. Who would believe it?"

At the bank, Michael met privately with one of his own superiors to explain what Tessa had discovered, and then called Tessa in. She related again what Blake had told her, then handed over the two photographs she had, both the one from college and the one taken outside Harry's Bar, and told them all she remembered of Tim Heslop. Promising to take care of the gun, they returned her passport. The backpack, cut open to retrieve the gun, was beyond further use.

Michael walked with Tessa afterward, down to where she could catch a taxi. As always the financial district in Singapore seemed busy. People pressed past them on the sidewalk, and the traffic on Robinson Road was predictably constant.

Michael didn't seem to notice. "Now the hard work begins," he said. "It will take a while to sort through all his work to locate the fraudulent loans."

She nodded.

"So I'm not sure when I'll be free," he said. "Not for a few days at least."

She could sense the tension in him. "Michael?"

"It's just this," he said, then broke off. A muscle jerked in his cheek, and she sensed an almost desperate control in the set of his jaw.

This, from Michael—her Michael, who always knew the right thing to do?

"What is it?" she said.

He took her hand in his. "Jillian said you were thinking about leaving today. Can you stay a little while, in case the bank decides to pursue this? They might need your help."

She gripped his hand, felt herself sinking, yet she couldn't let them part, not again, not without speaking.

"Tessa?"

She swallowed, gathering her courage. "Michael, listen to me. I have to say this. When Blake made me take my passport, I thought that was it, that he would kill me. And I realized, except for you, no one would have noticed, not really." She made a face. "I do tend to pick up and leave places pretty abruptly. Half the time my parents don't even know where I am."

He would have spoken, but she shook her head, still not finished.

"And I didn't want to go, Michael. That's what I realized. I don't want our lives to go in different directions. I want that deeper friendship that you talked about."

His grip on her hand tightened. "Do you know what you're saying?"

"Yes, I do. Will I stay? I will. I promise. As long as you want me to."

"Tessa…"

"I mean it: as long as you want."

The caution in his eyes wavered, with something strong and free and brilliant threatening its place. "Give me the option," he said, "and I might ask you to stay for a while." He hesitated. "Maybe even forever."

She gave a shaky laugh. "I hope you do."

He shook his head, still a little stunned. "I'll hold you to that. But you might as well know, you crazy girl, I would have come after you anyway. Even if none of this had happened, whatever it was that changed your mind, I wouldn't have given up this time. Not a chance."

"I'm glad, Michael, more than you can know."

He glanced around at the busy street, looked back at her, and groaned. "You crazy, incredible, wonderful woman." He kissed her briefly on the lips, but with a passionate intensity she couldn't mistake, then stepped back and away from her. "Later," he said. "Now you'd better go."

NINETEEN

The bank's security officers tried to track Blake's departure from Singapore. Unfortunately, no one under the name of Blake Hoffman or Tim Heslop had flown out of Changi Airport on that Monday, so presumably Blake had used another identity to ensure his escape.

Michael worked late into the night, both Monday and Tuesday, sorting through Blake's records.

"Will you be able to find him?" Tessa asked when he called Tuesday night.

"The bank has hired a stateside detective agency that specializes in white-collar crime, but they don't offer much hope. Too little, too late. It would be better, the head of the agency said, to do a little systematic checking up front. I wish I had taken your warning more seriously."

"But they don't blame you?"

"Without your intervention, it looks pretty clear he would have gotten away with much more. So, far from hurting my career, I'm coming off as a hero—thanks to you."

"I'm glad," she said.

"On that note, I think I might be able to get away tomorrow evening. Can we have dinner together? Sample some of Mrs. Ling's cooking?"

"Okay," she said, and gave a shaky laugh. "I'd like that."

As she had so often during the past days, after hanging up, she traced the butterfly on her new black cap. She had put herself into his care, a butterfly no longer poised for flight.

What did he have planned for her now?

∼ ∼ ∼ ∼ ∼

After work the next afternoon, Jillian grabbed a soft drink from the kitchen, flopped down full-length on the couch, then gave Tessa her customary rundown of what was happening at the bank.

"I can't tell, you know, whether they're putting Michael through the wringer because they blame him, or whether he's stepped forward to take the brunt of the work because he feels responsible."

"He says no. They're glad Blake left before he did worse damage."

Jillian propped herself on an elbow so she could see Tessa more clearly. "I hear he's taking a break tonight so he can have dinner with you. Is that why you're dressed up?"

Tessa glanced down at her periwinkle jumper and white tee. "Does it look that way?"

Jillian laughed. "Wear a ballgown or a burlap bag, it won't make any difference to Michael."

And when he showed up, Tessa could see Jillian was right. He looked too tired to notice anything. "Ready? Good." He leaned past Tessa into the doorway. "I'd come in and say hi, Jillian, except if I sit down at all, I doubt I'd be able to get up again."

"So get going already," she shot back.

Alone in the elevator with Tessa, he leaned against the side wall so he could watch her, his gaze warm and intent. "It's better than champagne, seeing you again."

His weariness seemed to be fading by the minute.

She lowered her head and smiled, hopeful and nervous and a little uncertain.

She asked about his day. He said something in response. Neither was paying much attention to words. The air seemed charged somehow, and when he touched her elbow briefly as she passed through the door of Jillian's building, he pulled his hand away with a quick audible breath.

From there, they walked in sedate silence to Michael's apartment building, making polite conversation to the neighbor who rode up in the elevator with them, neither looking at the other again, neither touching.

In his apartment, he closed the door and leaned back against it. "Hungry?" He sounded a little breathless.

She shook her head. "Not too." She couldn't seem to stop smiling.

"If you can wait," he said, "for dinner I mean, I have something to show you."

"Okay." She cleared her throat and pointed to the living area. "Should I sit on the couch?"

"Yes. Do. I'll be right back."

He returned with several large binders, which he piled onto the coffee table, and took a seat beside her. Incredibly, he looked a little nervous. She bit back laughter, born of joy and hard to control, and nodded toward the binders. "What are these?"

He pulled the top one onto his lap, but left it closed. "You asked me once how I knew you would want to see the petrochemical plant. Do you remember?"

"Yes."

"This is how I knew. I've been following your work. Shortly before I came to Singapore, about three and a half years ago, I subscribed to a clipping service. For a fee, they send me copies of everything you publish."

"My work?" Tessa held a hand to her chest. "Michael—everything?"

He gave a rueful smile. "It started with guilt, for breaking off our engagement so abruptly. I knew at the time it was for selfish reasons, and I suppose, in the beginning, I wanted to prove that ending the engagement was worth it—for your sake, I mean." He rubbed his forehead and groaned. "Now I think probably I was hoping as well to see you fail and come running back to me. I'm sorry."

"All my work?" she said. "You have everything?"

"Everything published. Seeing it come in, it didn't take me long to realize just how special your talent is. I can understand why people want to hire you." He pulled the first book over onto her lap. "Let me show you."

Page after page, each article and photograph and advertisement was meticulously preserved and dated. As she looked, he pointed out his favorite pictures. When they came to her stock photo of the married couple facing away from each other, she crossed her arms. "There it is, the picture itself."

He winced. "You can see why it's been on my conscience. But to be honest, at that point, when you were explaining stock photography to me, I would have been happy to have you describe how to plunge a toilet, just to hear you talk."

"A toilet?" She grinned.

"It's true. I've been in bad shape since I first saw you across the Hyatt Regency lobby all those weeks ago." He set aside the books and, after drawing her closer, pushed a strand of her hair, very, very gently, behind her ear. "I knew then that nothing had changed, Tessa. I still love you. I always will."

He pressed a long, warm kiss into her palm, then lifted his gaze back to hers. He looked cautious, even worried, and yet Tessa couldn't seem to summon enough breath to respond.

"Four years ago," he continued, "I thought you were wonderful, so alive and creative and energetic, but now..." He gave her hand a shake. "Tessa, say something. Do I have a chance?"

"Oh, Michael, of course I love you. I thought I made that clear on Monday, offering to stay."

He gripped her upper arms. "And you'll marry me?"

"Yes, if you want me to." She grabbed his tie and pulled him closer. "But you better mean it, Michael Lawton, because there's no going back this time."

His lips met hers with a fierce eagerness, and he held her so tightly she wondered for one crazy moment if she might suffocate. How strange, she thought dreamily as she returned his kisses, clinging just as tightly: her instinct for survival seemed to have completely vanished.

Later, after eating Mrs. Ling's delicious food, they sat side by side on the sofa.

"I'm sorry about Jillian," he said. "Sorry, of course, for what she went through, but sorry as well for putting you through so much confusion."

Tessa laughed. "I'm not. Wondering what you felt about her banished all question of what I felt about you. Do you think there's a chance for her?"

"You mean spiritually? Yes, I do. There's a streak of goodness in her that I truly believe comes from God. She was raised in the church. God can bring her back."

"I'm glad."

He pressed a kiss against her forehead. "I had it all planned, you know, while you were in Australia. Things had finally settled down with Jillian. I could put that behind me, get on with trying to win you back. I figured, Sunday to recuperate, and then dinner on Monday evening with flowers, candy, even the bended knee. Think what you missed."

"I missed you," she said, "for four long years. I just never let myself admit how much."

She sat back to get a better look at him. So much of her

future had been filled in for her—Michael waiting at the altar, his hands holding their first child, his voice praying at so many family meals, his smile from the pillow beside hers to greet her each morning. She reached a hand up to touch his face.

"I dreamed about you during those years," she said. "I thought I saw you on the streets or in airports, in the most out-of-the-way places. Wishful thinking, and always a disappointment. You don't know how many times I considered dropping by Mom's apartment in Japan while you were there."

"I wish you had." He held her close again. "But I want to know: what made you come to Singapore, anyway? And don't say the assignment. I didn't believe that reason at the Hyatt Regency, and I won't believe it now. So, come on, Tessa, let me have it."

"No one else appealed to me. It was beginning to bother me, especially since I was sure you couldn't possibly measure up to my memories." She laughed. "Silly me."

"And what made you change your mind? About leaving, I mean."

"Lots of things: what Simon said in the temple, and Jillian's concerns about God, and Blake going off in such a rush, and Li Hua, too. But most of all God. I thought I knew what he wanted. I was wrong."

"I have something for you." Michael pulled a small box from his pocket and set it in her hand. "I bought this four years ago, the week after you left Japan for that big assignment in China. I tried, I really did, to take it back. I even tried to find someone else to give it to. No chance."

She held the box out, open palm, toward him. "Open it, Michael."

He laughed. The box held a beautiful pearl ring flanked by two small diamonds. After slipping the ring on her finger, he lifted her hand to his lips. "I can't begin to tell you, Tessa, how grateful I am. Before God, I'll try never to give you cause for regret."

"Oh, Michael, me too."

"And I want you to know," he continued, "that I won't ever ask you to give up photography, not again." He laid her hand palm to palm on his own and stroked it gently. "When you left me in Japan, it's true, I resented your work—very much, because it had taken you from me. I thought myself so much in love that I couldn't survive weeks on end without you." He grunted. "I had no idea then what love meant. I wanted you with me, on my terms, for my benefit, and if you weren't going to comply—" He lifted eyes full of regret to her. "I'm sorry."

"It was the wrong time for both of us," Tessa said. "I still wanted to travel. I would have made you miserable. But, and it took me a while to realize this, the right decision then isn't the right decision now. I want a home, and children—children I take care of, not someone else—and a church where people know me. I do. And I want it all with you, Michael. I'm ready."

"And yet you must keep working, Tessa, at least on some level. I know that now, especially after seeing your incredible worldwide-church pictures. God gave you your talent. He's pleased with what you do, and I will be, too."

She hugged him to show how much she appreciated what he was saying, then shook her head. "Other things will please him just as well, Michael, and maybe even more—loving a husband, serving him, raising children to praise God. Like Li Hua said, sometimes it's the opportunities we set aside for his sake that bring him the most glory."

"That's true, but on this I'm determined, though I don't know how I'll manage while you're gone." He traced the contours of her face, as if learning its shape, then smiled and kissed her. "Some of your trips, at least, we can do together. I'll be your assistant, handing you the right lenses and distracting your subjects when you need that. Or if you'd rather, while you're piggybacking your camera gear, I'll piggyback the baby."

"Together. And a baby. Oh, Michael!"

She leaned her head against his chest, her heart full to the brim. It was just what she had told Jillian. They weren't going to need deals, she and Michael, bartering and negotiating with neither of them ever quite satisfied. As she was with God, she and Michael were at last reconciled, free to love and be loved in a relationship based on trust and hope and faith in God. And whatever happened in the future, whatever disagreements and troubles awaited them, they would face them together with a desire to please that grew out of a heart of love.

It was an assignment she hoped would never end.

Dear Reader:

Four years ago, world-class photographer Galen Rowell came to speak at Millikin University, where my husband teaches chemistry. I loved Mr. Rowell's pictures and admired his stories, but what inspired me most was the obvious regard he felt for the people he met in his travels. As I researched this book, I saw that same generosity in the work of other photographers, including Lisl Dennis, Susan McCartney, and especially Peter Menzel. His book *Material World* was a project Tessa would have loved to be involved in.

As for Singapore, I have long been intrigued by the setting, especially as it relates to the freedoms a holy God gives us and the necessity for grace this inevitably entails. From freedom and grace the story led naturally to the reason for both—the priority God places on a relationship with us.

In your own life, whatever world-class role God has chosen for you, may you always be assured of your importance to him and the significance you have in his kingdom.

To God alone be the glory,

Marilyn Kok

Write to Marilyn Kok
c/o Palisades
P.O. Box 1720
Sisters, Oregon 97759